4

Saint Francis of Assisi

PHOTOGRAPHS BY DENNIS STOCK
TEXT BY LAWRENCE CUNNINGHAM

A Scala Book, Published by Harper & Row, Publishers, San Francisco

Cambridge, Hagerstown, New York, Philadelphia, London, Mexico City, São Paulo, Sydney

Photographs are courtesy Dennis Stock (pp. 3, 5, 7, 8, 81-95); Scala, Florence (pp. 2, 4, 6, 17-24, 41-48, 50, 52, 54-56); Frick Collection, New York (p. 49); Bildarchiv Preussischer. Kulturbesitz, Berlin (p. 51); Giraudon, Paris (p. 53). Color plate captions appear on page 125.

All translations of excerpted material are by the author, unless otherwise noted.

FIRST EDITION

Library of Congress Cataloging in Publication Data

Stock, Dennis.
SAINT FRANCIS OF ASSISI.

Bibliography: p. 110.
1. Francis, of Assisi, Saint, 1182-1226.
I. Cunningham, Lawrence. II. Title.
BX4700.F6S69 1981   271'.3'024 [B]   81-47419
ISBN 0-06-061651-2   AACR2

81 82 83 84 85 10 9 8 7 6 5 4 3 2 1

The Canticle of Brother Sun

Most High, omnipotent, good Lord
To you alone belong praise and glory,
Honor, and blessing.
No man is worthy to breathe thy name.

Be praised, my Lord, for all your creatures.

In the first place for the blessed Brother Sun,
who gives us the day and enlightens us through you.
He is beautiful and radiant with his great splendor.
Giving witness of thee, Most Omnipotent One.

Be praised, my Lord, for Sister Moon and the stars
Formed by you so bright, precious, and beautiful.

Be praised my Lord, for Brother Wind
And the airy skies, so cloudy and serene;
For every weather, be praised, for it is life-giving.

Be praised, my Lord, for Sister Water,
So necessary yet so humble, precious, and chaste.

Be praised, my Lord, for Brother Fire,
Who lights up the night.

He is beautiful and carefree, robust, and fierce.

Be praised, my Lord, for our sister, Mother Earth,
Who nourishes and watches us
While bringing forth abundance of fruits with colored flowers
And herbs.

Be praised, my Lord, for those who pardon through your love
And bear weakness and trial.
Blessed are those who endure in peace,
For they will be crowned by you, Most High.

Be praised, my Lord, for our sister, Bodily Death,
Whom no living man can escape.
Woe to those who die in sin.
Blessed are those who discover thy holy will.
The second death will do them no harm.

Praise and bless my Lord.
Render thanks.
Serve him with great humility.   Amen.

Excerpts from the Rule of Saint Francis (1221)

The whole idea of the life of the brothers is to follow the example of Christ by a life of obedience, chastity, and freedom from all material possession. Here is our rule:

"If you wish to be perfect, go, sell all that you have, give it to the poor, and you will have a treasure in heaven. Then, come and follow me!

"If anyone wishes to follow me, let him deny himself, take up his cross, and come follow me.

"If anyone wishes to follow me and does not hate his father, mother, wife, children, brothers, and sisters—even his own life—he cannot be my disciple.

"Everyone who leaves father or mother or brothers and sisters or wife and children or house and property for love of me will get back a hundredfold and will inherit eternal life."

Anyone inspired by God to follow our way of life should be welcomed by the brothers. If he seems to be serious about joining us, the brothers should take him right away to one of the superiors without inquiring into his background. The superior, in turn, should make him feel welcome and give him encouragement while fully explaining our way of life. If he decides to stay, then he should quickly sell all his possessions and give everything away to the poor.

The brothers who have already promised obedience may have a habit with a hood, another without one if they need it, a belt, and some underclothing. Everyone should wear castoffs patched with sacking and other rags with the words of the Lord as an encouragement for them: "Those who dress in precious robes and seek delights and clothe themselves in soft garments are found in the palaces of kings."

Brothers, no matter who they might be, should avoid administrative positions such as chancellors or managers of large households. No job that they do take should ever be a source of scandal. They should seek the most humble jobs so that they are on the lowest rung of the economic ladder. They should be servants rather than masters.

Brothers who have retired to hermitages or other such places should never think of those spots as their own. They should grant hospitality to anyone who approaches, whether friend or enemy, thief or evildoer. If the brethern are gathered for a meeting, they should be hospitable and cheerful. There should be no hypocritical appearance of poetry or asceticism. In short, they should be happy, joyful, and gracious as befitting followers of the Lord.

The Lord says to "hold yourself free from every malice and evil desire; be on guard against the desires of this world and the cares of this life." Thus, under no condition is a brother to handle money in any form. He is not to use it to buy books or clothes or to accept it as payment for work. To put it bluntly, he should never handle money except to care for a sick brother. The true brother values money no more than a pebble; in fact, if he values money as much as a pebble, he is running a real risk. It would be a terrible thing for those who have chosen the road of abandonment to lose the whole kingdom of heaven for such a trivial thing.

The brothers who are anxious to follow the humility and poverty of our Lord Jesus Christ should allow themselves only what the Apostle permits: "Having food and something to cover ourselves with, we consider ourselves content." The brothers should consider it a privilege to live with the outcasts of this world: the sick, the weak, the poor lepers, and the beggars on the road. When the need arises, they are to beg without any sense of shame, remembering our Lord, who "set his face like a flint stone" and was not ashamed. Jesus, like Mary and the disciples, was a poor man and a wanderer; he was not above accepting charity. Even when the brothers are rebuffed, they should remember that God will turn their shame into honor. Shame falls on the one who causes it, not the one who must endure it.

Saint Francis on Himself

To me, Brother Francis, the Lord thus gave the grace to do penance: when I was still a sinner, I thought it too bitter a thing to look at lepers, and the Lord led me to them and taught me to be merciful; after leaving them, that which seemed bitter now appeared as sweetness both for soul and body. I tarried a bit and then left the world. In the churches the Lord gave me such faith that I was able to pray simply and say, "We adore you, Lord Jesus Christ, here and in all the churches of the whole world, and we bless you because by your holy cross you have redeemed the world."

The Lord then gave me, and grants me today, a great faith in the priests who live according to the usage of the church because of their holy orders, and even if they persecuted me, I would have recourse to them. And even if I were to possess the wisdom of Solomon and were to come upon the poor priests of this world, I would not preach in their churches if they were unwilling to have me. I would continue to love, honor, and respect them as well as other priests. They are my superiors. I wish to see no sin in them, for in them I see the Son of God, and they are my lords. And I act thus because I see nothing with the eyes of the body in this world of the most high Son of God except the body and blood which they receive and administer to others. I wish that these exalted mysteries be honored, venerated, and maintained in precious places. Anytime that I have found the holy names or the sacred writings in indecorous places, I have wished to gather them in decent places, and I wish that others will also do the same. Thus we should honor and venerate all theologians and others who dispense the Word of God as those who give spirit and life.

When the Lord had entrusted brothers to me, nobody told me how to treat them; but the Most High revealed to me personally that I ought to live according to the norm of the Holy Gospel. I had it all written in a few simple words, and the lord pope approved it. And those who wished to embrace this life gave the poor everything they had and contented themselves with a tunic patched inside and out and a belt and some underclothes. And we did not wish anything more.

We clerics recited the Office just as other clerics do and the lay members recited the Lord's Prayer; we remained with alacrity in the churches. We were simple and subject to all. And I did manual labor and wished to do it; I hope that all the brothers will do honest work with their hands. Those who are not skilled in work should learn not in order to gain a good wage for their effort but in order to give a good example and avoid idleness. When the reward of work is not forthcoming, we return to the table of the Lord in begging door to door.

The Lord has revealed to me that we ought to give the following greeting to others: "May the Lord give you peace." Let the brothers beware of accepting churches, poor inhabitations, or other constructions made for them unless they conform to the demands of holy poverty, as we have promised in the rule to live always as wayfarers and pilgrims.

I make it an imperative demand of obedience that no brother dare accept any privilege from the Roman Curia, either by himself or through an intermediary, for a church or any other place using the pretext of the needs of preaching or a refuge from persecution; rather, if they are not received, let them flee to another area and there do penance with the blessing of God. I wish firmly to obey the minister general of this brotherhood and whatever guardian it pleases him to appoint over me. I want to be a slave in his hands, not moving or acting in the least manner without his wish, for he is my master. And even though I am weak and simple, I want a cleric with me always to recite the Office with me, as it is established in the rule.

In a similar manner all the other brothers are obliged by obedience to obey their guardians and to recite the Office according to the rule. And if anyone is found who does not say the Office according to the rule, or who varies it or who is not Catholic, let all the brothers, wherever they may be, be held in obedience to turn that brother over to the guardian of the place that is nearest to them. And that minister is to watch him night and day as a prisoner in bonds until the moment when he can turn the brother over to his own minister. And the minister is bound by obedience to watch him night and day like a prisoner in bonds and have him escorted by brothers to the lord of Ostia who is the master, protector, and corrector of the whole brotherhood.

No brother should say, "This is another rule"; for this is a testament, a memorial, an exhortation, and a remembrance that I, the little Brother Francis, have made for you, my blessed brothers, so that you will better be able to observe the holy rule that we have promised before the Lord. The minister general and all the other ministers and guardians are obliged by obedience to neither add nor subtract from these words. In fact, they should carry a copy of this along with the rule, and in all the meetings when they read the rule, this always should be read. All my brothers, clerical and lay, are ordered in obedience to make glosses neither on the rule nor on these words; neither should they say, "They should be interpreted thusly"; rather, as the Lord told me what to say and how to write this rule purely and simply, they are to observe this rule and these words simply and purely and fulfill them right to the end.

Whoever has observed these things will be filled with the heavenly benediction of the Most High Father and on earth be filled with the blessing of his beloved Son and the Most Holy Spirit, the Paraclete, and all the heavenly powers and the saints. And I, Brother Francis, your little one and your servant, inasmuch as I can, will strengthen you within and without with this most holy blessing. Amen.

The last testament of Francis of Assisi.

Portraits of Saint Francis

No saint in Christendom has been portrayed more frequently than Francis of Assisi. A full-length figure in Subiaco, near Assisi, shows Francis without a halo (page 17). From this we can infer that it was painted before Francis was canonized by Pope Gregory VIII in 1228.

The following eight illustrations show how, during the 100 years after his death, five artists portrayed the face of Francis.

17. Detail from a full-length fresco portrait; Monastery of the Sacro Speco, Subiaco (Umbria); Anonymous (1228 or earlier).

18. Detail from a panel painting of *St. Francis between Two Angels*; Saint Mary of the Angels, Assisi. This anonymous thirteenth-century artist frescoed the first cycle of stories from the life of Saint Francis beginning in 1230, only four years after the death of Francis.

19. Detail from the panel painting *St. Francis*; Diocesan Museum, Arezzo; Margaritone d'Arezzo. This painter, mentioned in a document of 1262, often painted the likeness of Francis. This panel is signed Margarit de Aritio.

20. Detail from the panel painting *St. Francis of Assisi*; Saint Mary of the Angels, Assisi; Cimabue. Cimabue was mentioned by Dante as being Italy's finest painter before he was surpassed by his pupil, Giotto. According to tradition (and to an inscription on the panel itself), the panel was originally used to cover Francis's coffin.

21. Detail from a fresco of *The Madonna Enthroned with Angels and St. Francis*; Lower Church of St. Francis, Assisi; Cimabue. It is interesting to compare these two paintings of Saint Francis by the same painter. A certain amount of retouching was done over the years, but it has been largely eliminated by a recent cleaning. The two paintings have been dated between the years 1275–1286.

22. Detail from the fresco *Francis Gives His Cloak to a Poor Knight*; Upper Church of St. Francis, Assisi; Giotto. It is generally accepted (though still disputed by some art historians) that Giotto was responsible for the vast cycle of frescoes depicting the life of Francis in the upper part of the great Franciscan basilica in Assisi. Here the young Francis does not conform to the traditional iconography of the saint but is portrayed as a local youth dressed in the latest style of the 1290s, when this fresco cycle was undertaken.

23. Detail from the fresco *Francis Preaching to the Birds*; Upper Church of St. Francis, Assisi; Giotto. This depiction of the kindly saint among his beloved animals has strongly influenced the more popular iconography of Saint Francis.

24. Detail from the fresco *The Death of St. Francis*; Church of Santa Croce, Florence; Giotto. Here Francis, again an ordinary young man, is recently deceased. The fact that he is shown without a beard may be the result of instructions from church authorities, who at that time were concerned to render the saint's image, as well as that of his order, more acceptable to the established church.

17

18

19

22

23

24

The Life of Saint Francis

IT IS difficult, when writing about the life of Saint Francis of Assisi, to avoid writing about a stereotype. After all, his very name brings to mind sermons to birds, tamed wolves, simplicity of life, genial friars padding about flower-filled cloisters, and swallows unfailingly returning to the picturesque mission of San Juan Capistrano. That image of Saint Francis of Assisi is best—or worst—summarized by those concrete statues of the saint with a dove perched on his shoulder that are offered for sale by suburban garden centers around the country. That Saint Francis is meant to nestle innocuously among the backyard rosebushes near the birdbath.

That image of the saint, largely inherited from the neo-medieval impulses of nineteenth-century romanticism, derives from a certain verifiable tradition about Francis. Like all stereotypes, however, it flattens out or erases other aspects of his personality. It is difficult to think of the "Little Poor Man of Assisi" as a center of bitter contention, the source of radical social impulses, or the inspiration for a fierce and unyielding asceticism. Yet, for many, Francis was one or all of those things in his own lifetime and after his death. In fact, when one goes beyond the usual romantic clichés about Saint Francis, one discovers a person who, for all of his transparent attractiveness, is complex to the point of enigma.

The complexity of Saint Francis derives partly from his own personality (saints are never simple persons), and partly from historical sources. He left posterity very few writings (one brilliant vernacular poem, a few prayers, some terse letters, and a number of rather jejune Latin documents about the Franciscan Order and its way of life), and we depend for information largely on the various *legenda* written after his death for the use of the pious who wished to know about the saint, his life, and, especially, his miraculous powers. These documents, some of them filled with a deeply moving charm and piety, are colored by fiercely partisan polemics, pious elaborations, and a certain cavalier attitude toward historical accuracy that is endemic in medieval hagiography. Thus scholars must search for the historical Francis through the writings of others.

The early biographies of Saint Francis are called *legenda*, but that word must not be equated with our modern term *legend*. *Legenda* derives from the Latin verb *legere*, "to read," because these early lives of Francis were meant to be heard read in liturgical services on feasts of the saint and other solemn occasions. Despite their tendency to preach and moralize, they are an invaluable source of knowledge. Some were written by persons who knew the saint personally; other writers based their accounts on the collected memories of his oldest and closest companions. These stories reflect a deep historical core about Francis. At least one of them, a beautiful fourteenth-century Italian collection called *The Little Flowers of Saint Francis*, has attained the status of a literary classic.

The "true" Francis may never be recovered fully (what person in history ever is fully known?), but it is unlikely that historians will or should give up the search. The fact is that the figure of Saint Francis has transcended the historical facts of his existence. Francis has become the font of a long tradition of art, letters, and sentiment, a paradigm of authentic religious living, and a model of spiritual excellence. At that level, one can speak of Francis as both man and myth.

Saint Francis was born Giovanni Bernadone in either 1181 or 1182 in the Italian hill town of Assisi. His parents, Pietro and Pica, were members of the rather well-to-do merchant class of the town. Pietro Bernadone was away in France when his son was born. On his return, he had the boy's name changed from Giovanni to Francesco ("The Little Frenchman"—perhaps a tribute to France, a country he loved and from which his wife's family came).

Of the youth of Francis we know very little. He probably received a bit of rudimentary schooling from the priests of his parish church of San Giorgio. He spoke and sang in French, a language he probably learned at home. Later accounts of his life emphasized his recklessness and frivolity as a youth. "Until he was nearly twenty-five he squandered his time terribly. Indeed, he outshone all his friends in trivialities, suggested various evils, and was eager for foolishness of every kind," wrote his first biographer, Thomas of Celano. That this style of life is plausible should not surprise us, given his position as the spoiled son of a wealthy mercantile family.

In 1202, Francis marched with the gentlemen soldiers of Assisi to engage the army of the city of Perugia. It was probably one of those bloody skirmishes that the medievals loved to call a war. At any rate, Francis was captured in battle and imprisoned in Perugia. He spent a year there until his father could negotiate the price of his ransom. For Francis, as it has been for many, incarceration proved to be a turning point. We don't know what his prison routine was like or how he reacted to it, but when he returned to Assisi he spent a year in convalescence. He also began to change as a person. By 1205 he had left his home to take up a life of solitude. He gradually adopted the traditional garb of a hermit (thick shoes, a tunic with a belt) and lived near a tumbledown and nearly abandoned church at the edge of Assisi called San Damiano. In obedience to voices he heard in the church, he began literally to "rebuild the church." With his own hands he began to repair the ruined walls of San Damiano.

Between 1206 and 1208, Francis continued to live this marginal existence. The period was also marked by episodes of remonstrance and quarrels with his father. Pietro may have been indulgent of Francis's adolescent high jinks, but he was absolutely livid about this new kind of life. Outraged by the squalor of his life and his prodigal generosity to the poor, his father even tried to imprison him in the cellar of the family home. It was, after all, Pietro's hard-earned money that Francis was giving to the poor and leprous of the city. Finally, in an act of desperation, he hauled his recalcitrant son before the local bishop to demand that justice be done. This fateful encounter between father and son has been immortalized in frescoes both at Assisi and in the Bardi chapel of the church of Santa

Croce in Florence. Giotto's inspiration for his version of the encounter must have been drawn from Saint Bonaventure's *Major Life* of the saint:

His father brought Francis before the bishop of the diocese. He wanted Francis to renounce all claims and return his goods. Because of his love for poverty, Francis readily agreed to come before the bishop. With no urging, hesitation, justification, or speech he took off his clothes and gave them to his father. It was discovered that he had on a hairshirt under his costly robes. He even took off his pants in his zeal so that he stood naked before the bishop. To his father he said, "Up to today I called you father but now I can say in all honesty *Our Father who art in heaven*. He is my patrimony and I put my faith in Him." On hearing this the bishop was dumbstruck at his zeal. He jumped up to embrace Francis while covering him with his own cape. He got his servants to bring him some clothes. They got an old smock which had belonged to a farmer. Francis put it on after drawing a cross on it with a piece of chalk. He judged it a worthy garment for a beggar and follower of the Crucified Christ. Thus, the Most High's servant was stripped of all possessions; he could now follow his Lover who once hung stripped on the cross. . . . Free of all earthly bonds Francis left the town and sought for quiet places where he could be alone in solitude and silence to hear the secrets which God could reveal to him.

On February 24, 1208, Francis was at Mass in the little church of Saint Mary of the Angels when he heard these words from Saint Matthew read out at the proclamation of the Gospel: "Take no gold or silver or copper in your wallet, no bag for your journey, nor two tunics or sandals or a staff. . . ." This Gospel message gave Francis a new direction. He decided to put aside his life as a hermit to begin an itinerant existence after the command of Christ. If the period from 1205 can be called the time of his first conversion, then this day (it was the feast of Saint Matthias) must be understood as the moment of what William James, in *The Varieties of Religious Experience*, has called "the second conversion." Francis saw that his calling was to live in absolute poverty, wandering through the towns and villages preaching the Gospel.

By this time, Francis had attracted some followers who desired to share his life. What was this life to be? Francis had a very simple plan: to live as the great masses of the rural and urban poor—the *popolo minuto*—lived. To them he would preach the Gospel. This simple plan, however, was not without risk. The medieval church took a dim view of unsupervised bands of evangelical itinerants who identified too closely with the proletarian masses. Too many groups had been stirring up revolutionary expectations, and the church authorities were not indifferent to their presence.

Francis understood that he needed church approval for his little group. In the spring of 1209, he wrote a rule of life, since lost, and then set off for Rome together with his small band of brothers. They finally gained an audience with that most redoubtable of medieval pontiffs, Pope Innocent III. Although later accounts of the meeting are filled with papal dreams and initial rebuffs, the basic fact is that Francis got his rule approved and found a friend in Cardinal Hugolin of Ostia, who became the band's protector. Near the end of his life, Francis himself gave a laconic and characteristically self-effacing account of all these events in his *Testament*:

> When the Lord entrusted brothers to me, nobody told me how to treat them but the Most High revealed to me personally that I ought to live according to the norms of the Holy Gospel. I had it all written down in a few simple words, and the lord pope approved it. And those who wished to embrace the life gave the poor everything they had and contented themselves with a tunic patched inside and out, and a belt and some underclothes. And we did not wish for anything more.

Francis and his first companions then embarked on a life of wandering and preaching. His constant theme was conversion to the values of the Gospel. He taught his early friars to greet everyone with the salutation "Peace and good!" To realize how passionately Francis wanted that theme to be preached and accepted, we must recover some sense of the violence and carnage of the age. Blood vendettas, legal mutilations, city strife, incessant war, and murder were part and parcel of everyday life. Medieval towns, located on tops of hills, were girded by thick walls and filled with bastions and heavily fortified homes to protect the citizenry in an age when roving bands of mercenaries, rapacious political tyrants, and family brawling were the order of the day.

From the time of the papal approbation until 1220, the life of Francis was one of incessant wandering punctuated with periods of withdrawal into solitude. We hear of him wandering all over Italy, and of his visits to Spain with an idea of penetrating the Moslem world as a missionary. He was almost certainly in Rome for the Fourth Lateran Council in 1215. In 1219, Francis sailed for Acre and Damietta to make contact with the Moslem world once again. It is a mark of his incredible personality that he was able to cross the Crusader lines and visit the sultan Maliak el Kamel who, despite his admiration for the Christian holy man, did not decide to convert. Visitors to Assisi today can still see the carved ivory horn that the sultan presented to Francis as a memento of his visit.

It was during this eventful decade—in 1212, to be exact—that Francis received Clare Favarone, a well-to-do young lady of Assisi, into his way of life. She was to be the foundress of the "Second Order," now known as the Poor Clares, of Franciscans. On Palm Sunday in 1212, Francis cut off her long blonde tresses (lovingly preserved in Assisi), dressed her in penitential serge, and sent her to live at San Damiano, along with some other members of her family who had joined her. The brothers had taken up their residence at the little church of Saint Mary of the Angels (where Francis had heard the Gospel about the life of poverty) in the valley below the town of Assisi. Over that little chapel of Saint Mary's (or the "Little Portion," as it is called) now stands a huge late-baroque church. It is a colossal monument to good intentions and execrable taste.

The relationship of Francis and Clare (she was to outlive him by years and become on her own a powerful figure and counselor to popes) is the story of a great spiritual friendship. A wonderful account in *The Little Flowers of Saint Francis* (the so-called *Fioretti*) underlines this kinship of spirit. Although it reminds us almost instinctively of the great mystical vision of Saint Augustine and Saint Monica recounted in Book IX of *The Confessions*, this story of Francis and Clare is far more "Franciscan" in its simplicity and naiveté:

When Saint Francis was in Assisi, he often visited Saint Clare in order to give her spiritual counsel. She had a great desire to eat with Saint Francis and had asked him many times, but he never granted her this consolation. Some of his companions came to Saint Francis once to talk about the desire of Clare and said to him, "Father, we do not think that this rigidity is in keeping with divine love. You do not want to grant such a little thing as a meal to Sister Clare, a virgin who is so holy and so beloved of God. It was through your preaching that she abandoned the world and her riches, and that should be kept in mind. Even if she were to ask a greater favor, you ought to grant it since she is your spiritual offspring."

Saint Francis said, "Do you think then that I should grant her request?"

His friends said, "Yes, father. She is worthy of this grace."

Saint Francis then said, "If it seems good to you, then it seems good to me. It would be better for her to come here to Saint Mary of the Angels, for she has been cloistered so long at Saint Damian's and it would be pleasing to her to see again the place where her hair was cut and where she became a bride of Christ. So, in the name of God, we will eat here."

When the time came Saint Clare left her convent with a companion and accompanied by the brothers of Saint Francis. When she arrived at Saint Mary of the Angels, she devoutly saluted the Virgin Mary at the altar where she had been first veiled and tonsured. Then she found a place to wait until the hour of the meal.

In the meantime Saint Francis prepared a meal and spread it on the ground, as was his custom. When the hour came Saint Francis sat with Saint Clare, his companion sat with hers, and the other brothers humbly ringed themselves around the table. With the first plate Saint Francis began to speak softly and persuasively and wonderfully of God. The grace of God descended on the whole company, and shortly they were all rapt in the contemplation of God.

While they were so rapt with their eyes and hands reaching toward the heavens, the citizens of Assisi and Bettona and the people in the environs of Saint Mary of the Angels saw the church, the land, and the forest around enveloped in fire. The citizens of Assisi ran to the place to put out the blaze, for they were convinced that everything would be lost in a holocaust. When they arrived there, they found nothing burning at all. Entering the place, they found Saint Francis and Saint Clare and all the others rapt in the contemplation of God while seated around a meager meal.

They understood immediately that the fire they saw was divine and not material. They were sure that God had made the fire appear miraculously so as to illustrate the fire of divine love which burned in the hearts of those holy brothers and nuns. They returned home happy and edified in their hearts. After a length of time Saint Francis and Saint Clare came to their senses, and they were so filled with spiritual food that they had no appetite for the meal before them. So that finished the meal, and Saint Clare, well accompanied, returned to Saint Damian's.

When the sisters saw her coming back, they were overjoyed, for they were afraid that Saint Francis may have been ready to send her off to be head of another convent, as he had sent Sister Agnes, the blood sister of Saint Clare, to govern the convent of Monticelli in Florence. Saint Francis had once said to Saint Clare, "Be prepared should I need to send you to some other place." And she, as true child of obedience, had said in reply, "Father, I am ready to go wherever you wish to send me." It was for this reason that the sisters were so happy on seeing Saint Clare coming back to them to stay.

In the praise of Christ. Amen.

Throughout the years of 1210 to 1220, the number of followers of Saint Francis grew at a truly incredible rate. By 1217, we know that small bands of the *fratres minores* ("little brothers") lived in Italy, France, Spain, Bohemia, Germany, England, and the Holy Land. By 1219, missionaries had been sent to Hungary and to what is today Morocco and Tunisia. Lay folk who wished to share in the life of the Franciscans were provided with a modified rule of life and were enrolled in what had been called the "Third Order."

We have an independent eyewitness who testifies to the power of these early friars and the example of their lives. In 1216 a French bishop, Jacques De Vitry, visited the papal court in Perugia. Pope Innocent III had just died (De Vitry records that his body had been stripped of its robes and jewels by thieves who broke into the church while the pope was lying in state, a comment on the times), and Francis's protector, Cardinal Hugolin, had succeeded him as Pope Gregory IX. De Vitry says in a letter from Perugia that the papal court, with its intrigues, law suits, political squabbles, and money grubbing, "saddened me greatly." Amid the depressing sights at the court, however, he was consoled to find "persons of both sexes, rich and worldly, who have renounced their possessions and, for the love of Christ, turned their backs on the world. They are called 'Friars Minor' and 'Little Sisters.'" De Vitry went on to observe that they were indifferent to the honors of the world but passionate in their desire to convert people to the following of Christ.

Growth inevitably brought problems. It was one thing for a relatively small group of wandering brothers to subsist by the work of their hands or to get their living through begging, but it was quite a different matter when that small band grew into the thousands. The saint could always ask the Father in heaven to "give us this day our daily bread"; but the superiors, good men all but not necessarily saints, had to feed and house large numbers of friars.

There was the further question of education. Francis wanted his friars to live simply and among the poor. How was he to handle the ever-increasing number of educated persons who begged admittance to his order? He resisted the idea of his friars attending the universities that were then in their first period of growth and expansion—indeed, one legend even has Francis cursing a group of friars who had opened a hospice in the university town of Bologna. Francis must not have been entirely opposed to learning, however, since in a letter of disputed authenticity he gave Saint Anthony of Padua permission to teach the friars theology as long as it did not "extinguish the habit of prayer."

Francis was most concerned about any possibility of mitigating his simple but unbending concern for evangelical poverty. We catch a sense of this urgency in the plea that he makes in his *Testament*, which he wrote sometime in the final years of his life:

No brother should say "This is another rule"; for this is a testament, a memorial, an exhortation, and a remembrance that I, the little Brother Francis, have made for you, my blessed brothers so that you will be better able to observe the holy rule that we have promised before the Lord. . . . All the brothers clerical and lay are ordered in obedience to make glosses neither on the rule or on these words; neither should they say "This should be interpreted thusly"; rather, as the Lord told me what to say and how to write this rule simply and purely, they are to observe this rule and these words simply and purely and fulfill them right to the end.

Whoever has observed these things will be filled with the heavenly benediction of the Most High Father and on earth be filled with the blessing of His beloved Son and the Most Holy Spirit, the Paraclete, and all the heavenly powers and the saints. And I, Brother Francis, your little one and your servant, inasmuch as I can, will strengthen you within and without with this holy blessing. Amen.

In 1220, Francis resigned as head of the order of friars. Others would now deal with the daily exigencies of organizing his burgeoning movement. In those final years, however, he was almost plaintive in his desire that the friars not depart from the primitive standards he had set for them in the first years. These years, harried as they were by his concern for matters within the order, were also years of great consolation and spiritual creativity. The year 1223, when a definitive rule for the order was finally approved by the pope, found Francis in the town of Greccio for the celebration of Christmas. In order to intensify and dramatize the real poverty of the first Christmas, Francis decided to celebrate the feast in a setting like that described in the New Testament. He found a cave near the town and attended Mass amid the animals traditionally associated with the feast. This celebration was to mark the beginning of the now almost universal custom of building and adorning manger scenes in churches and homes. At the celebration, Francis read the Gospel and preached (the saint was never ordained to the priesthood but he was a deacon) to the assembled faithful. Thomas of Celano's *First Life* provides a glowing account of the scene at Greccio:

The joyful day came with great happiness. The friars came from their different places. Neighborhood people prepared with joy according to their capacity, bringing candles and torches to illumine the night that has been the light for the world through its star. Finally, the saint of God arrived and saw it and was glad. The manger was ready, hay was spread, and the ox and ass led in. Thus, simplicity was honored, poverty exalted, humility praised. Greccio was made a new Bethlehem. The night became as day to the joy of men and animals. The people were happy at this great mystery. The forest echoed with the voices of the congregation; the rocks cried out in jubilation. The friars sang their debt of praise to God and the night echoed with their hymns. The saint of God stood near the manger, overwhelmed with love and swelling with happiness. . . . The gifts of the Almighty were distributed there as a holy man in the congregation saw a vision. He spied a child lying in the manger and he saw the saint go to the manger and rouse it from sleep. This vision was a fitting one for the infant Jesus has been forgotten by a number of people but through the merits of Saint Francis he was brought back from sleep and the scene was etched in the memory of many. Finally, the solemnities of the night were over and each returned joyfully home.

The following year, 1224, Saint Francis decided to go into retreat at Mount LaVerna, a desolate mountain in Tuscany that had been given over for his use by a noble of the district. It was there on that mountaintop retreat on September 14th (the Feast of the Exaltation of the Holy Cross) that Francis had a mystical experience that left him with wounds on his hands, feet, and side similar to those of the crucified Christ. The impression of the stigmata, widely reported in the lifetime of the saint, was the first instance of this kind reported in the Christian West. The idea of a person actually carrying wounds on his body similar to those of Christ had an immense impact on the medieval imagination. It was a scene painted over and over again: from the primitive panels of the Duecento, through Giotto, to the ineffably beautiful Bellini *Ecstasy of Saint Francis* (now in the Frick collection in New York) done at the end of the fifteenth century. The literary source for these depictions is the brief description of the event given in Bonaventure's *Major Life* of the saint:

One morning around the feast of the Holy Cross while he was at prayer on the mountainside Francis saw a seraph with six flaming wings coming down from heaven. The vision descended speedily and hovered in the air over him. He saw the image of a crucified Man in the middle of the wings with stretched out hands and feet nailed to a cross. Two of the wings (of the seraph) were pointed above the head, two flew, and two covered his body. Francis, struck dumb by the vision, reacted with joy and sorrow: joy at the gracious look Christ gave him from among the wings of the seraph and sorrow like a sword thrust that pierced his soul at the sight of the figure affixed to a cross. . . . As the vision receded from sight it left the saint's heart ablaze and imprinted upon his own body a miraculous likeness. Right then the marks of the nails began to appear in his body . . .

The intensity of that mystical experience did nothing to improve the already failing health of the saint. Francis suffered from chronic infections of the eyes (contracted, perhaps, during his visits to the Middle East), which had been treated by the excruciatingly dubious therapy of cauterizing his temples with white hot irons and piercing his ears with iron needles. From 1225 until his death on October 3, 1226, he made sporadic journeys (often riding on a donkey because of his weakness) interspersed with rests in Assisi. In the spring of 1225, he collapsed while visiting Saint Clare at her convent of San Damiano. He stayed at a cell there to regain his health. It was in that convent that Francis composed "The Canticle of Brother Sun," one of the first vernacular poems in the Italian language.

"The Canticle" was probably meant to be sung by the friars as they went about their preaching tours to the villages and cities. Despite its simple lines, it is a highly complex work that echoes the canticles of the Bible, Francis's own profound sense of the presence of God in the world, and his deeply felt conviction that the world, in its own manifold beauty and variety, is itself a hymn of praise to God. The lines that Francis wrote at San Damiano are these:

THE CANTICLE OF BROTHER SUN

Most high, omnipotent, good Lord
To you alone belong praise and glory
Honor, and blessing.
No man is worthy to breathe thy name.

Be praised, my Lord, for all your creatures.

In the first place for the blessed Brother Sun
who gives us the day and enlightens us through you.
He is beautiful and radiant with his great splendor,

Giving witness of thee, most omnipotent One.

Be praised, my Lord, for Sister Moon and the stars
Formed by you so bright, precious, and beautiful.

Be praised, my Lord, for Brother Wind
And the airy skies, so cloudy and serene;
For every weather, be praised, for it is life-giving.

Be praised, my Lord, for Sister Water
So necessary yet so humble, precious, and chaste.

Be praised, my Lord, for Brother Fire,
Who lights up the night,
He is beautiful and carefree, robust and fierce.

Be praised, my Lord, for our sister, Mother Earth,
who nourishes and watches us
while bringing forth abundant fruits with colored flowers
and herbs.

Later in the same year, Saint Francis was able to reconcile the bishop of Assisi and the mayor of the town who had been feuding. In honor of that reconciliation, Francis added some additional verses to the "Canticle":

Be praised, my Lord, for those who pardon through your love
And bear witness and trial.
Blessed are those who endure in peace
For they will be crowned by you, Most High.

Francis spent his last days in the care of Bishop Guido of Assisi. It was at the episcopal residence that Saint Francis added some final verses to his poem:

Be praised, my Lord, for our sister, bodily death,
Whom no living man can escape.
Woe to those who die in sin.

Blessed are those who discover thy holy will.
The second death will do them no harm.

Praise and bless the Lord.
Render him thanks.
Serve him with great humility. Amen.

Francis died at the palace of the bishop of Assisi with his brethren in attendance. Tradition has it that they sang the "Canticle" at his deathbed. Francis himself requested that he be put on the ground, his beloved Mother Earth, so he could wait for Sister Death. The following day, October 4, 1226, his body was carried to the church of San Giorgio, after a stop was made so that Saint Clare and her nuns could bid him a last farewell. Two years later—exceedingly fast by Roman standards—Pope Gregory IX (his old friend and protector Cardinal Hugolin) came to Assisi for the canonization proceedings. In 1230, his body was transferred from the church of San Giorgio to a massive crypt under the Romanesque church of Saint Francis, which had been built by funds raised through the energetic work of Brother Elias of Cortona, the head of the order. Thus, the Little Poor Man of Assisi who, like his Master, wished to live without a place to rest his head, now reposed under a great fortresslike church decorated in the intervening years by masterpieces of painting executed by such masters as Cimabue, Giotto, Simone de Martini, and other painters of the early Italian Renaissance. Later generations could not quite imitate him fully in his desire for Gospel poverty, but they were able to offer him something that he could have appreciated: the gift of beauty.

Even a life as poetically beautiful as that of Saint Francis does not fully explain the immense impact he had on his own times. The life of Saint Francis triggered an outpouring of religious and aesthetic emotion of such magnitude that it is now a commonplace among scholars to reckon his influence as absolutely basic in catalyzing the Italian Renaissance. Furthermore, Saint Francis was one of the few figures in the history of the Catholic tradition of saints who has been claimed as one of their own by those outside the Roman communion. Indeed, Paul Sabatier claimed that Francis was one of those figures, like Michelangelo and Goethe, who transcend cultural boundaries to achieve universal acclaim for their human genius.

It may be that the *persona* of the saint (and it is his person and not his writings that is crucial) gives us some small clue to his universal appeal. He stood as a living sermon to the people of his own time and, by extension, to our own. His life was not charming; it was prophetic. The great Viennese medievalist Friedrich Heer has trenchantly underscored this prophetic side of the life of Francis. In *The Medieval World*,* Heer notes how the life of Francis stood as a rebuke to the prevailing cultural forces of his day. Francis reminded the heretical Cathars, active in Southern France, that humans are not "pure spirit" but flesh and blood people who live on this earth. To the papacy, then at the apex of its political and social power, he preached the notion of the Christian as servant, not ruler. To the bloodletting crusaders and the bellicose Italian tyrants, he was the symbol of the blessedness of the peacemaker. To the brutal "realists" of the day, his message was one of humility, kindness, courtesy, and love for the meanest of creatures. To those who would etherealize Christianity into a foggy platonism, Francis brought home the reality of the passion and crucifixion of Jesus. To the rapidly emerging middle class of Italy, he warned of the poisonous effects of greed and speculation.

Francis delivered this prophetic message without the bitterness of the fanatic. It was the veracity of his life, not the sharpness of his tongue, which made his message so clear. The serious edge to Francis's prophetic style was all the more effective for its directness, simplicity, and lack of guile. Francis combined a rigorous Christian faith and a spirit of simple goodness. How could anyone not love a man who could express sentiments like this one, preserved by some of his oldest companions and friends:

Many times we remember him saying that if he had a chance to speak to the emperor he would persuade him to pass a law obliging every person to scatter corn and other grains on the roads and in the fields outside the towns at Christmastide so that the birds, especially our sisters the song birds, would have an extra ration. This would be done in honor of the Son of God

---

* Friedrich Heer, *The Medieval World* (New York: New American Library, 1964).

because he was born poor and the Virgin had to lay him in a hay manger between an ox and a donkey.

Because of the sheer beauty of his personality Saint Francis, unlike many other saints, evoked intense interest about himself as a person. It was not the power of his intellect or his miraculous powers that attracted people to Francis, as was the case with the theologian Saint Bonaventure or the wonder-working Saint Anthony of Padua. Nor was he an emblematic figure without personality, like the semi-mythical Saint Christopher. His contemporary, Saint Dominic, who founded the Order of Preachers, or Dominicans—the other great mendicant order of the period—never triggered the imagination of the artist or poet in quite the same manner that Francis did, despite his religious genius and the influence of his order. Francis was unique.

Francis's early biographers even took the time to tell their readers what the saint looked like—something rather rare in hagiography, unless it were done for homiletic reasons—and one can take this fact as a piece of evidence about the interest in Francis as a distinct and living person. Since this book provides a number of portraits of the saint (although none were executed from life and are, as a consequence, idealized) it is not inappropriate to end this essay on the life of the saint with some words written about the features of Francis to complement the visual images of him that art has provided. In the *First Life*, Thomas of Celano writes:

He was of medium height and almost close to shortness. His head was of moderate size and roundish; his face long and well defined. His brow was smooth and low with eyes that were black and healthy; he had black hair and straight eyebrows. His nose was even and straight, his ear, small and straight, his temples unmarked. He had a strong, sweet, lyrical, and clear voice while his manner of speaking could be peaceful yet fiery and direct. He had even, white teeth, a thin pair of lips, and a beard which was black but not curly. He had a slender neck, straight shoulders, short arms, delicate hands, long fingers, thin legs, and small feet. He was a thin man, with delicate skin, but he wore rough garments, slept very little, and was of a most giving nature . . .

ALITER·B·F·FVIT·DENV̄TIATVS·A·XP̄ OTF̄ŌMA·PEREGRINI·QVOD·DEBEBAT· NASCI·SICVT·IP̄S·ĪSTABLO·QVALT·OVIDĀ·FATVV·P̄STĒNEBR̄A·BĒ·VEST̄INER·IN

43

50

Lady Poverty and Mother Earth

BECAUSE Saint Francis of Assisi emphasized poverty of life and had a great love of the natural world and its beauty, there is almost an irresistible urge to depict him as a charming *naif* with simple tastes and a Wordsworthian sense of nature's refinements. Such a view is attractive, but it falsifies the uniqueness of the saint. His love was not for nature. In fact, he never used such an abstract noun. He was a lover of particularities. As G. K. Chesterton once pithily noted, Saint Francis did not want to see the woods for the trees. Nor was Saint Francis interested in simplicity of life. He was interested in poverty, and that is quite another thing.

There is a distinct relationship between Francis's love of poverty and his love for the created world, even though such loves seem, at base, paradoxical. Francis was not a lover of poverty and a lover of the world and a follower of the Gospel, as if these were discrete interests. To understand Francis is to understand that his most conspicuous virtues were all of a piece. Ultimately, they were all connected with his desire to follow the Christ of the Gospel as closely and as completely as he could. It was in Christ's poverty, however, that Francis thought he had found the more perfect way to live in the imitation of Jesus Christ.

Poverty is a much used and a much abused word. It is also an extremely relative term. The poverty of the worst ghetto in America cannot be equated with the poverty of the worst ghetto in Calcutta. Nor is it just to describe the starving as poor. They are what Mother Teresa calls "the destitute dying"; to call them poor is to diminish their plight. Simple humanity demands that we use the words "poor" and "poverty" with care, otherwise their reality is diluted.

Simplicity of life and poverty are not the same. There are many people who live very simple lives, either by choice or circumstance, who are not poor. Poverty does not mean simply a lack of money or goods. In its essence, poverty means radical insecurity about the basic means of life. Poverty is literally not knowing where the next meal is coming from, or the frantic fear of getting ill because there is no money for a doctor, or the gnawing despair when one recognizes the gap between the next possible time when money will come and the actual needs of the household. It is, in short, a knowledge that the world is not solid, secure, and benign. Poverty is not only want; it is the fear and dread that derives from want.

The sense of radical insecurity that the poor struggle against is the insecurity that Saint Francis sought. Indeed, he sought it in joy and not in dread. Why?

For Saint Francis, living in the radical insecurity of poverty was the ultimate act of living faith in the providence of God and the promises of Christ. It was the acting out in life of the Gospel command to "be not solicitous of what you shall eat or what you shall wear . . . does not your heavenly Father know you have need of these things?" (Matt. 6:25-33). All the worries that Saint Francis expressed about what the friars were to possess, where they were to live, how they were to avoid money, the acts of charity they were to perform, must be seen against this basic desire to live completely under the aegis of God's care and providence. The unseemly squabbles about the interpretation of the life of poverty, following the death of Francis, often missed this point. The question was not whether there were to be stone houses or wooden houses, whether there were to be books or no books. The radical question was this: in the possession or the use of things, was there a denial of the providential care that God would have over them? Francis was not interested in a style of life; he was interested in a radical act of faith. Confusion over that point has muddied much of the discussion about the nature of Francis's attitude towards poverty.

Francis, true to his deepest poetic instincts, described this attitude towards a life of faith in poverty by borrowing from medieval romance literature. Francis conceived of his life as a wooing and wedding of Lady Poverty:

> People thought he wished to get married so they asked him, "Francis, do you desire to marry?" But he answered, "I shall take the most noble and beautiful wife you have ever seen. She will surpass every other woman in beauty and wisdom." Indeed, the spotless spouse of God is the true religion which he married. It was the hidden desire of the kingdom of heaven which he sought so ardently . . .

Within two years after his death, an anonymous book called *The Sacred Romance of Blessed Francis and Lady Poverty* appeared. The *Sacrum Commercium*, to give it its Latin title, filtered through radical Franciscan literature in the thirteenth century, and was the inspiration for Dante's famous tribute to the saint and Lady Poverty in the *Divine Comedy*.

In canto xi of the *Paradiso*, Dante says that Lady Poverty had been deprived of a spouse for over a millennium (i.e., since the time of Christ), but Saint Francis was to be her new lover. It was in her lap that he was to die, and it was to her care that he entrusted his true followers. One particular line in Dante's poem is of particular significance. Simone Weil, the French mystic and writer, has called it the most perfect line in Dante's poem. Describing Christ and Lady Poverty, the poet writes:

Dove Maria rimase giuso
Ella con Cristo salse en sulla croce.
(While Mary stood below
  She [i.e., Poverty] ascended the cross with Christ.)

The close identification that Dante makes between poverty and the passion of Christ is a genuinely helpful insight into the deepest nature of the Franciscan concept of poverty. Francis's emphasis on the passion of Christ and his reception of the stigmata cannot be fully appreciated unless it is also seen in terms of his notion of evangelical poverty.

The poor life that Francis sought, a life lived with absolute trust in God's providence, was, after all, done in the imitation of Christ. Christ was not only materially poor. Indeed, the real character of Christ's poverty is existential. Christ, as Saint Paul reminds us in the *Epistle to the Philippians*, "emptied himself taking the form of a servant, being born in the likeness of men." This emptying (*kenosis*) was most perfectly expressed in the Passion and Death of Christ. It was on the cross that the radical insecurity of poverty was most perfectly expressed. It was on the cross, after all, where life itself was risked.

The notion of radical self-denial in the imitation of Christ was hardly new in the history of Christianity. The whole dynamic of martyrdom in the early centuries of Christianity was predicated on the notion that the martyr was acting after the manner of Christ who "gave up his life for his friends." The idea of radical self-giving does carry with it certain risks and temptations, the most notable of which is the temptation to turn self-denial into an aberrational form of self-loathing. Some of the early desert ascetics provide abundant examples of the ascetic ideal being carried to unhealthy conclusions.

It was the peculiar religious genius of Saint Francis that he could combine an utter seriousness with the following of Christ and a healthy love for the world as a gift from God. One does not find in Francis that morbid hatred of the self that unchecked ascetics often manifested. Francis called his body "Brother Ass," and he exerted considerable energies in subduing its recalcitrant demands, but he never allowed that discipline to degenerate into fanaticism. We know that he slept on the ground, ate sparingly, kept long vigils throughout the night, lived in cast-off clothing, and gave away everything that came into his possession. What we cannot visualize is a Saint Francis loaded down with chains, or a Saint Francis perched on a pillar. In fact, the *Fioretti* recounts that Saint Francis ordered his friars not to give way to fantastic penances and had various penitential instruments confiscated, since they caused injury and even death to overzealous but imprudent friars.

Saint Francis linked self-sacrificing suffering in the name of Christ not with sorrow but with joy. Perfect joy, as he once told his oldest companion Brother Leo, was the service of Christ in times when the world despised that service or rejected the person who wished to serve. It was perfect joy because it was perfect, self-effacing love.

The kind of poverty that Francis preached brought forth a paradoxical, but perfectly cogent, conclusion about the world we live in. If one lives purely in the providence of God and after the manner of Christ's self-emptying, one's awareness of the world as gift is sharpened. For Saint Francis, the world was both a sign of the presence of God in itself and—even more fundamental—a sign of God's free gift.

It is against this perfectly orthodox theological background that we must see Francis's great love for the natural world and its creatures. Francis was not a naturalist nor was he a nature mystic. Attempts to turn Saint Francis into a proto-ecologist are well-intentioned but tendentious; to make him the patron saint of the movement is a bit closer to the mark. Francis was a sacramentalist, which is to say he saw the visible world as a sign of the presence of God and, more specifically, of the presence of Christ in the created world.

One way to get a closer notion of Francis's notion of the proper relationship of the natural world to God is to look closely at his "Canticle of Brother Sun." A translator's *crux* in that poem sheds light on Francis's theology. When Francis wrote *Lodato si, mi Signore, per sora luna* how are we to translate the word *per*? Does it mean be praised *for* Sister Moon or be praised *through* or *by means of* Sister Moon? Either translation makes perfectly good sense of the Italian. One version means that Francis praises God for the gift of the moon, while the other asks the moon to join in the creation of the Creator whom Francis wishes to praise. Evidence in the early Franciscan literature suggests that different writers understood the term in different senses. There is also biblical evidence (the poem reflects the psalms and canticles of the Old Testament) to support either translation. Scholars have argued both cases strenuously, but it may be that Francis intended both senses in his text in a manner that cannot adequately be rendered in the English. In that double sense, the *per* means at once thanksgiving and instrumentality. Both notions are strongly present in the life of the saint.

For Francis, then, to see the world with the eyes of faith was to see the world both as a gift and as a sign of the suffused presence of Christ who redeemed the world. The point was well made by Saint Bonaventure in his *Major Life* of the saint:

The awareness that everything comes from the same source filled Francis with tremendous affection. He provoked him to call the most humble creatures brother and sister. He did this because he realized that they all came from a common father. He kept his most tender love for those creatures who reflect Christ's gentleness or are used in the Scriptures as figures of Him. He often rescued lambs who were to be slaughtered in veneration of the Lamb of God who offered His life for sinners.

Francis was incapable of seeing the world of creation as a mere thing for the use of humanity. He insisted on the integrity of all creatures in the scheme of things. This attitude has led one scholar to speak of Francis's essentially democratic view of the world of creation. Thomas of Celano preserves a command of the saint that captures this spirit perfectly:

He ordered the gardeners to leave the garden borders untilled so that the green of the grass and the beauty of the wildflowers in their season could herald the beauty of the Father of all things. He ordered a small plot to be set aside in the gardens for sweet smelling flowers so that people who saw them would be reminded of the sweetness of the Lord.

All of the early legends cite numerous anecdotes and sermons of the saint that testify to his love for the creatures of the world. He preached to the birds, reveled in the presence of beautiful flowers, protected and tamed animals, and, in the words of Thomas of Celano, "embraced them with rapturous devotion speaking to them of the Lord and encouraging them to praise their Creator." A small sampling of these anecdotes will give a flavor of the whole. The following are adapted from Thomas of Celano's *First and Second Life* of the saint:

A certain nobleman from Siena once sent [Francis] a pheasant when he was sick. He was delighted with the gift, not because he had intention of eating it but because he could rejoice in its beauty and thus intensify his love for the Creator. He used to say to the pheasant, "Praised be our Creator, Brother Pheasant."

Near the cell of the saint at Saint Mary of the Angels, a cicada used to perch in a tree and chirp out all day long. At times the blessed father would hold out his hand and call it to him, "Come to me, Sister Cicada." And she would fly right to him as if endowed with reason.

Even toward little worms, he had a great sense of love, for he had read in the Scriptures concerning our Lord, "I am a worm and no man."

When he would come on a vast field of flowers, he would preach to them and exhort them to praise God as if they could understand his words. He would likewise exhort cornfields, vineyards, stones, fields, springs of water, green plants in gardens, earth, fire, and water to a praise and love for the Creator. In short, he called all creatures by the name of *brother* and, in a manner that few can understand, he saw the simple things of creation with the eye of one whose heart had already attained to the blessed liberty of the children of God.

Francis's everyday relationship between the created world, its creatures, human-kind, and the Creator can best be understood by his use of the term *cortesia*. We use the word "courtesy" (*cortesia*) to mean manners. Originally, it meant the behavior and etiquette expected of one who served at a noble court. It was also used of those who behaved with the nobility expected of a knight, and was the preeminent characteristic of the knight in Chaucer's *Canterbury Tales*. For Saint Francis, who knew the courtly literature well and borrowed its conceits for his own purposes, the word *cortesia* took on a complex meaning. *Cortesia* and manners were not the same thing. *Cortesia* was a way of seeing and a way of acting towards others.

It is recorded that when the doctor brought the white-hot cauterizing iron towards him to treat his eyes Francis said, "I pray you, Brother Fire, be courteous to me." G. K. Chesterton remarked of that incident that it is the rare poet who remembers his poetry at a moment of agony or crisis. *Cortesia* is the recognition of rights, duties, gifts, and privileges as they exist in relationship. For Saint Francis, this concept extended not only to human relations but to all of creation. For Francis, even humanity and fire exist in relation; true *cortesia* exists in the recognition of that relation.

In the "Canticle of Brother Sun" the earth, our mother, is praised for bringing forth beauty in its flowering plants. The implicit notion in that simple observation is that the earth is courteous to us (it gives us beauty) and we, in gratitude, owe an act of courtesy to it. It is that mutuality in which Francis locates our relationship to the world, and which also prevents us from despising the world or its creatures.

Nowhere in Franciscan legends does this notion of *cortesia* come across so clearly as in the famous story of Saint Francis and the wolf of Gubbio. Mean-minded folk have read the story as a thinly disguised account of Francis pacifying a tyrant of the town. In fact, Francis did rein in a tyrant or two in his life, and those bloody despots were as fierce as wolves. So the wolf of Gubbio may have been a tyrant, but the poetry of the story permits us to read it as it is written in *The Little Flowers*:

While Saint Francis was staying in the town of Gubbio, there appeared a huge wolf. It was so ferocious and terrible that it devoured not only animals but also men. The citizens of the town were so terrified that they always went out fully armed as if ready to go to war. But, despite this, they were helpless, especially when a single man met the wolf. Because of their fear, nobody would even venture out of the house.

Because of this, Saint Francis (who felt great pity for the people) made up his mind to go and find the wolf, even though everyone told him not to. Still, making the sign of the cross, he went out one day with his companions, putting his trust in God.

His companions hung back, but Saint Francis took the road leading to the place where the wolf was often found. A number of people followed in order to see a miracle, and when the open-mouthed wolf approached Saint Francis, the saint made the sign of the cross over the wolf and called out to him, "Come to me, Brother Wolf, and I order you, in the name of Christ, neither to harm me nor the others."

Incredible as it seems, the moment Saint Francis made the sign of the cross, the wolf closed his mouth and stopped dead in his tracks. When he heard the order, he came meekly to the feet of Saint Francis and lay down.

Then Saint Francis spoke to him, "Brother Wolf, you have done much damage in these parts and committed great crimes by maiming and killing God's creatures without his permission. You haven't stopped at this but also maimed and killed men who are made in the likeness of God. You ought to be treated like a robber and a murderer and handed over to the hangman. The people hate and curse you, and this land is an enemy to you. But, Brother Wolf, I want to make peace between you and these people. If you will stop harming them, they, in turn, will forgive you, and neither men nor dogs will pester you in the future."

When Saint Francis said this, the wolf showed his agreement with the words of the saint by signaling with his body and tail and ears and with a nod of his head showed his compliance. Then Saint Francis said, "Brother Wolf, since you are ready to make peace and keep your word, I promise that these people will give you enough to eat during your life so that you need not starve. I understand that you did these evil things because of hunger. Since I have begged this favor, Brother Wolf, you must promise me to harm neither animal nor man. Do you promise this?" And the wolf, with a nod of his head, promised.

Then Saint Francis said, "Brother Wolf, I want you to give me a sign that you have promised so that I can have faith in you." Saint Francis put out his hand as a sign of their pact and the wolf lifted its paw and tamely put it in the hand of Saint Francis, giving the best sign of faith that he could. Then Saint Francis said, "Brother Wolf, I command you in the name of Jesus Christ to come with me without fear, and we can go and make peace in the name of God." And the wolf obediently followed him as a meek lamb would.

The citizens of the town were stupefied. The news spread everywhere, and in a moment the people—young and old, men and women—lined the piazza to see Saint Francis with the wolf. When Saint Francis saw the crowd, he stepped forward and began to preach to them. He told them that God permitted such evils because of sinfulness and that they should fear the pain of eternal damnation more than a wolf, who can only kill their bodies. He said that they should fear the opening of the jaws of hell more than the jaws of a simple animal. "Be converted, beloved of God, and do penance for your sins, and God will free you from the wolf today and the gates of hell tomorrow."

When he had finished his talk, Saint Francis said, "Listen to me, my brothers. Brother Wolf, who is here before you, has promised and sworn peace with you now and in the future; he will do you no harm if you will give him a bit to eat. And I promise that he will keep his end of the bargain." The people unanimously promised to feed him daily. Then Saint Francis said to the wolf, "And you, Brother Wolf, do you promise to keep the peace and not harm the animals or men or any other creature?" And the wolf, kneeling down with his head bowed, made signs with his tail and ears to indicate that he wished to keep the pact.

Saint Francis said, "Brother Wolf, I want you to make the sign of agreement that you made outside the city gate here among the people so that you will show that you will not betray the pact that I have made in your name." And the wolf put his right paw in the hand of Saint Francis. With this, and because of all the other things they had seen, the people began to praise God in the heavens for sending them Saint Francis and for freeing them from the ravages of the once wild wolf.

After this, the wolf lived in Gubbio for two years. He went daily from house to house without harm or being harmed. The people fed him and he was such a familiar sight that the dogs didn't even bark at him. Finally, after two years, Brother Wolf died of old age. The people mourned him, because he had been a familiar sight among them and was a constant reminder of the virtue and holiness of Saint Francis.

To the praise of Christ. Amen.

We have insisted that Francis's love for poverty was rooted in his reading of the Gospel, and that his love for the natural world was a direct outcome of his desire to live poorly under the providential eye of God. If that were all Saint Francis stood for, we would be correct in dismissing him as a sort of medieval Doctor Doolittle who talked to the animals. In fact, Saint Francis's love and compassion for animals and the natural world was only an extension of his compassionate love for his human brothers and sisters.

Francis's life reflects his great capacity for loving friendship. He was surrounded by an intimate circle of close companions. He had a loving friendship with women like Saint Clare and Jacopa Settesoli, he was a confidant of such powerful men as Pope Gregory IX, and he exercised his influence on a wide cross-section of the admiring nobility of the period. Only rarely did his anger flare, and then it was usually in connection with those within his own order who betrayed his high ideals. Thus to a friar who schemed to give his earthly goods to his family (instead of to the poor as Francis ordered) Francis gave the unflattering name of Brother Fly. Francis also cursed a superior who too lavishly appointed a house for the Franciscan brothers. In a fit of anger, Francis himself ejected the errant friars from the convent.

The saintliness of Francis, however, derives not from the loving concern he showed to the circle of his extended family, but from his ability to love those who are naturally unlovable. Francis, in his final *Testament*, dates his conversion to the moment when he changed his attitude about these people: "When I was still a sinner, I thought it too bitter a thing to look at lepers and the Lord led me to them and taught me to be merciful. After being with them, that which seemed bitter now appeared as sweetness both for soul and body."

What strikes one so forcefully abut that short passage is its specificity. Francis does not say that he learned to love humanity or mankind or even "souls." He learned to love those poor ragged figures who lived at the edge of most medieval towns segregated by law from the crowd of humanity, feared by everyone, and loathed even by themselves because of their wretched and little-understood disease. The care of the leper in much of medieval hagiography is a primary test of heroic Christian service. To give alms to poor lepers was charity; to speak to them was heroism; to fraternally embrace them was saintly.

Francis's capacity for this kind of very specific love for others was rooted in his apprehension of two fundamental biblical ideas. The first is the statement in Genesis that every person is made "in the image and likeness of God" (Genesis 1:26). The second is the New Testament refinement of that idea deriving from the fact that Jesus was the Son of God. The consequence of the Incarnation is that every person is ennobled and dignified by the fact that Christ became human and took on flesh. Every person is an image of Christ. To honor an individual is to honor that Christ who said that "whatever is done to the least person is done to Himself" (Matthew 25:40 and 45).

The contemporary novelist Elie Wiesel tells a wonderfully "Franciscan" story that he learned from Hasidic lore. A wealthy Jewish merchant treats a poor old man with rudeness and disdain as they travel together on a train. As they arrive at their common destination, the merchant finds the station thronged with pious Jews waiting in ecstatic joy to greet the arrival of one of the holiest *rebbes* of Europe, and learns to his chagrin that the old man in his compartment is that saintly *rebbe*. Embarrassed at his disgraceful behavior and distraught that he missed a golden opportunity to speak in privacy to a wise and holy man, the merchant pushes his way through the crowd to find the old man. When he reached him, he begs the *rebbe*'s forgiveness and requests his blessing. The old rabbi looks at him and replies, "I cannot forgive you. To receive forgiveness you must go out and beg it from every poor old person in the world."

Francis of Assisi had that same unswerving instinct for seeing the universal reflected in each person. He demanded that everyone look past the "unloveableness" of the individual to see the universal bedrock of human dignity elevated by the Incarnation of Christ. The Franciscan legends all recount his strenuous efforts to instruct others, especially his friars, in this regard and the following is found in a number of the early legends:

Once a certain friar cursed a poor man who begged alms, saying, "Perhaps you are wealthy and only pretend to be poor." Saint Francis, the father of the poor, heard this in sadness. He rebuked the friar for saying such a thing and ordered himself to strip off his clothes, prostrate, and kiss the feet of this poor man to beg his forgiveness. Francis used to say: "Whoever curses a poor man injures Christ whose image he bears since Christ made himself poor for us in the world." Frequently, when he found the poor carrying heavy burdens of wood or other loads, he would offer to shoulder the load in this same spirit.

It is important to emphasize that Saint Francis did not romanticize the state of the poor. Nor did he accept its widespread presence in his time with detached fatalism. He himself had chosen poverty voluntarily and for compelling spiritual reasons. He did not want others to have poverty imposed on them simply because he had elected to live in that fashion. At the same time, however, he never put himself in the role of social reformer. Saint Francis had no grand plan to war on poverty as a social phenomenon (nobody in his day did), nor was he a passionate preacher against the social reality of class poverty (some radical Franciscans later in the century did combine his radical style of poverty with an apocalyptic sense of earthly revolution). Late in the thirteenth century, some Franciscans looked for a "Third Age" to be ushered in after a spasm of violence, and saw Francis as the man who heralded the dawning of this age.

Francis himself had a much simpler and more direct vision of life: to aid the poor whenever and wherever he encountered them, with no accounting of the personal cost. Francis genuinely loved the poor, and was willing to be absolutely self-giving in their behalf. For Francis, this spontaneous and total giving to others was at the core of the Gospel.

It has often been said that saints like Francis of Assisi (or Mother Teresa of Calcutta today) put bandaids on hemorrhages, since they never attack the root causes of poverty and injustice to the poor. That is a woefully misplaced criticism. To be sure, there must be those who reflect on the large social issues of human misery. There must be attempts to modify or overthrow the structures that cause them. In Chesterton's analogy, people who engage in such laudable enterprises wish to see the forest, not the trees. The saints like Francis are called only to see the trees. They never have an overarching scheme or a master plan. They respond immediately to need as they find it. It is the individual as that individual presents him or herself to the saints that compels the gesture of service. The many stories told in the legends to exemplify the charity of Saint Francis to the poor have two things in common: Francis would give whatever was at hand for the alleviation of the poor, and he would give it immediately. One detects, in the many edifying vignettes about the saint's charity, a basic note of urgency untouched by any hint of self-conscious reflection. The person comes to the saint, states a need, and evokes an immediate response:

An old and poor woman who had two sons who were friars once came to Saint Mary of the Angels to beg alms from Saint Francis. The saint went to Brother Peter of Catania (who was the minister general at the time) and asked if there was anything to give the woman, adding that a mother of a friar was a mother to all the friars. Brother Peter answered, "The only thing in the house is a copy of the New Testament, which we use to read the lessons during the night office." Saint Francis said to him, "Give her the Bible; it will be more pleasing to God that she should have it than we should read from it." Thus, she got the first New Testament that the brotherhood had owned.

Once a poor man begged alms from Saint Francis. The saint had nothing at all to give him, so he got a knife and cut off part of his tunic to give to the old man, for he did not want him to go away emptyhanded.

Seeing a poor man's misery he said to his companions, "This man's poverty shames us and mocks our poverty." His companions asked him what he meant. The saint said, "I am mortified when I meet a person poorer than myself. I elected poverty and made her my Lady, my joy, and my spiritual and temporal treasure. God and humanity know that I profess to be poor. I am ashamed when I meet someone who is poorer than me."

Saint Francis often repeated the words: "I was never a thief. I mean that alms given to us as the inheritance of the poor have always been used most sparingly so that I would not defraud the genuine poor. To act to the contrary would be theft."

The total vision of Saint Francis starts with the Christ of the Gospel and ends with that same Christ. Francis felt that he could intuit Christ in the world and in others. He burned to imitate Him as closely as he could in his own life. It may well be that Francis's simple Christocentric piety is the reason why he is one of the few genuinely ecumenical saints in Christianity. Anyone who has spent any amount of time at Assisi cannot but be impressed by the numbers of Protestants and other non-Roman Catholics who come there not as day-tripping tourists, but as pilgrims. In that city, with its enchanting countryside and its soft pink stone (quarried from nearby Mount Subasio, where Francis often retreated in prayer) and its stunning eminence on a hill, people sense the sacramental presence of God so readily perceived by Francis. There is a universal appeal in all of this. It may not be insignificant that in my own hometown the one church that is under the patronage of the Poor Man of Assisi is Episcopalian and not Roman Catholic.

Saint Francis's wide appeal to all Christians is not an invitation to characterize him as anything other than what he was: a medieval Catholic. Saint Francis was neither a proto-Protestant nor a nondenominational Christian. Anyone who is at all familiar with the saint's life will immediately recognize that nowhere does he criticize the Church, no matter how much its excesses and deficiencies pained him. Francis recognized that excessively zealous reformist groups in his own time (like the Poor Men of Lyons or the followers of Peter Waldo) often ran afoul of the Church and ended as groups emarginated from its larger social fabric. Francis, in fact, often affirmed his complete loyalty to the Church. In his final *Testament*, Francis makes it clear that affirmation of loyalty was not merely a strategy; it was a grace that God granted him:

> The Lord then gave me, and gives me today, a great faith in the priests who live according to the usages of the church because of their Holy Orders, and even if they persecuted me, I would have recourse to them. And even if I were to have the wisdom of Solomon and were to come up on the poor priests of this world, I would not preach in their churches if they were unwilling to have me. I would continue to love, honor, and respect them as well as other priests. They are my superiors. I wish to see no sin in them, for in them I see the Son of God, and they are my lords.

The Middle Ages put a high premium on sanctity, and it was recognized that Francis sought that sanctity with unswerving singlemindedness. The early legends of his life had no other intention than to show him as a searcher and finder of a way to completely identify with Christ. Even the polemical slant of some of those early documents (to bolster fidelity to the original ideals of the saint against more lax interpretations) was intended to show that others should follow the example of this imitator of Christ. For these writers, it was not important that Francis spoke to animals; it was important that he saw those animals as reflecting the goodness of God's creation. If Francis lived in the leper colonies, it was because God gave him the strength to do so. If people were converted, gave away their goods, or radically changed their lives, it was because Francis was a saint. In other words, the early writers of the Franciscan legends were not interested in the life of Francis as such. They were interested in Francis the imitator of Christ. "In him," writes Saint Bonaventure in the preface to his *Major Life* of the saint, "we can contemplate the lavish mercy of God. The example of the saint urges us away from worldly thoughts or appetites and towards a life in Christ who is both our happiness and our hope."

We do not live in the world of Saint Francis. Is there any way to appropriate something from the life of a man who had visions and mystical experiences and who demanded fidelity to an organized church? What, in short, is a person to do with the figure of this man?

One possibility is to sanitize his image by a process of demythologizing him for the modern taste. That is not only a difficult task but a destructive one. Even on the grounds of aesthetics, it seems to be a falsification to disentangle Francis from the naive stories of the *Fioretti* or the simple *exempla* of the legends or the primitive force of the early painters of Tuscan Italy in the thirteenth century. To undertake such a process would either end up being hopelessly reductionistic or clinically false. We cannot extract a disembodied essence from a living historical person.

If we cannot appropriate the spirituality of Francis as it is, there is another way to view him that would be both faithful to his memory and useful for our own time. We need simply ask what the elements are that perdure over and beyond the medieval packaging in which they arrive to us.

I would say that the most significant fact about the character of Francis's sanctity was his ability to be utterly serious in his search for God, without losing a sense of generosity and human scale. He was an utterly serious person, which is quite different from being an utterly fanatical one. To say that Francis is serious seems, at first blush, to be paradoxical. The sanitized Francis appears to be whimsical, lighthearted, and gentle. Such a characterization is, it seems to me, derived from a too facile attempt to sanitize or sentimentalize his person. There is another side to Francis: the Francis who is totally dedicated to a life of poverty, prayer, and ascetic discipline. It is the story of utter self-giving, inexhaustible searching for the meaning of love and sacrifice. It is the story of a God-haunted man.

It was a serious commitment, not a whimsical notion, that changed a frivolous young playboy into the blind, ragged figure of the saint. It was seriousness about his model, Christ, that allowed him to work or beg or wander or embrace the poor. Poverty was not an affectation or a protest. It was an imitation of the One who shed the glory of heaven to "take the form of a servant."

To those in the Church, the seriousness of Saint Francis is a sign of contradiction. The seriousness of Francis has a prophetic bite to it. He demands that the church person understand the full consequences of the New Testament imperative to "put on Christ." To put it another way: saints like Francis are a reproach (in the deepest biblical sense of that term) to those who would live as Christians without seriousness. The peculiar insight of Francis was that Christianity is not made more credible by rearranging the institutional furniture. Structural reform, liberalization of traditions, or impulses for democratization will not move people to kiss the outcasts in today's world, nor will they show us how to bless peace, tame the wolf of war, or confront the image of Christ in every human being.

No Christian can ask for the meek Francis without getting the suffering one. Meekness and sacrifice are both facets of the Christ whom Francis wished to imitate. One cannot sustain a love for the world without understanding the One from whom the world derives.

Someone once said that Christianity had not been tried and found wanting. It never had been tried. Saint Francis, in his seriousness, did try it and did not find it wanting.

If Saint Francis provides a prophetic reproach for the contemporary Christian, he also provides a puzzle for the non-Christian and an enigma for the nonbeliever. The life of Saint Francis raises an interesting question. He led a life that reflected some extraordinarily attractive characteristics. He was a man profoundly concerned about peace. He acted as a mediator and pacifier. He was passionately devoted to reconciling rich and poor, men and women, human beings and the natural world. His compassion was lavished on the poor and his sense of beauty was constant. He was quite ready to risk all for love.

There is hardly a person alive today who cannot identify with those qualities of life. We are all sensitive to the quality of our natural surroundings, just as we hope and pray for the end of racial and social strife. A larger awareness of the world's problems creates for all of us a sense that forces tear at the very fabric of what we call civilized life.

In a similar vein, we have not lost our thirst for some overarching pattern that helps us explain who we are, where we are going, and what the very fact of existence means or does not mean. Whether we find the answers in ideology or religion, the desire for meaning seems never to be assuaged.

If we are to be serious about our world and its meaning, then it seems that we have need of those who live their lives with a sense of seriousness. If we are to understand the enormity of our personal or social problems, or if we are to see ways to act and live, then we must have models and paradigms who show us what crisis is and how we are to respond to it.

Is that not what saints and heroes have always done? It seems eminently fair to say that we needed the Mahatma Gandhis and Martin Luther Kings to show us the power inherent in the rejection of violence, just as we needed concentration camp survivors to tell us how depraved humans can be and what price we pay for acquiescence to depravity. Is not the Jewish writer Elie Wiesel correct when he says that the survivor's task is to tell stories so that the world will remember? Is it not correct to say that the simple yet ineluctable *nyet* of Aleksandr Solzhenitsyn is a more powerful indictment of totalitarian ideology than all the volumes of propaganda that the world has produced? Is it not true, in short, that it is the serious people who rise up in our midst who truly show us the way?

If the above is a fair statement of the power of saints and heroes, then we are left with a simple question: does Francis the saint speak to us today?

In the life of Saint Francis, as we discern it from the early writings and the early art, we can detect elements that belong exclusively neither to his age nor to our own. They are elements that are beyond culture, even though culture speaks of them in particular ways. They are questions about life itself: life and love, suffering and death, beauty and ugliness, gentleness and fierceness, poetry and prayer. In that sense, to range over the medieval world of Francis of Assisi is to see ourselves in our aspirations and our needs. They are as simple as the beauty of Mother Earth and as broodingly mysterious as Sister Death.

The first and most immediate way in which the life of Francis reaches the modern sensibility is through natural beauty. It is impossible not to react almost spontaneously to Francis's love for the natural world. No one would think of filling the pages of books on the lives of Saint Augustine or Saint Thomas Aquinas with sensitive photographs of scenery. It does seem natural and perfectly appropriate, however, to thus illustrate a book on the life of Saint Francis.

It is not merely Francis's love of creation that attracts us. It is that deeper quality, given to a very few saints and some artists of genius, to make us see the world with a fresh eye. The late Paul Tillich, the great Protestant theologian of culture, once remarked that there was more religion in one of Cezanne's apples than in all the conventional religious painting done at the end of the last century. What Tillich meant, I think, is that Cezanne had a genuine capacity for communicating the mysterious, ever-fresh density of reality. Cezanne made us really look at the world. That is a very Franciscan quality. It is also a greatly needed gift.

When one speaks about the need for beauty or the great desirability of a "fresh" eye, it is easy to dismiss such arguments as so much overly refined aesthetic twaddle. Beauty is nice, but it has nothing to do with the nuts and bolts of the real world. It is a poetic extra. In fact, one could argue that it has everything to do with the real world both at a philosophical and a social level.

The ability to appreciate the beauty of the world and to see it fresh negates—in that very vision—the ability to tolerate ugliness, to turn a blind eye to cruelty, and to remain passive as beauty disappears. We are only now learning, much to our pain and considerable chagrin, that the intentional act of creating ugliness (think of much of our public housing for the poor) or the passive act of tolerating the destruction of the beauty that we possess does, in fact, dehumanize us, individually and socially. At a far deeper level, the conflict of beauty and ugliness is patent. There is bitter ugliness in the face of a starving child and ineffable beauty in the face of a healthy one.

The pallid cliché "decline of the quality of life" does not begin to encompass the deep wounds that eyes accustomed to ugliness inflict on us. Saint Francis would fully agree with Dostoevsky's observation that "beauty will save the world." Dostoevsky's dictum is not an aesthetic manifesto; it is a program of life rooted in a religious vision of the world.

An eye for beauty, the life of Francis teaches us, brings with it a corollary: a deeply existential attitude of gratefulness. It is one of those curious paradoxes common in the spiritual experience of Christianity that Francis felt more grateful as he became more poor. Poverty never reduced his sense that both the world and his own existence were a gift.

By its very nature, a gift carries with it two qualities: the intention of the giver and the enrichment of the recipient. Those gifts we most cherish are those which most persistently remind us of a loved giver. We attach a "sentimental value" to such gifts that goes beyond market value. To live fully is to cherish the gift for itself and in full recognition of the giver.

For Saint Francis, God is the perfect giver because He is the gift. God gives us the world, life, and, for Francis the Christian, "His only begotten Son." The beauty of the world and the intrinsic dignity of every individual is guaranteed by its rootedness in God. To understand that fact prevents one from ever calling Francis a pantheist; Francis did not mistake the gift for the giver. *The Legend of Perugia*, an early source for the life of Francis, records some apposite words of the saint in this regard:

He also said: "An artist who depicts the Lord or the Blessed Virgin honors them and presents them to our imagination. Still, the painting can make no other claim than being a thing created from wood and paint. God's creature is like that painting in that it is something created through whom the creator is honored. A creature must not claim any more honor than the paint and wood of the painting. Honor and glory go to God alone . . ."

To understand the theological context behind Francis's love for nature and his desire for the poor life is the best safeguard against either trivializing or sentimentalizing the meaning of his life or his message. When Saint Francis was in retreat on Mount LaVerna in 1224, the year in which he received the stigmata, he once asked Brother Leo to bring him some paper and ink so that he could write down for him some praises of the Lord upon which he had "meditated in his heart." Brother Leo kept that parchment on his person for years (as its present battered and creased condition clearly shows), and it is now preserved as a precious relic of Francis at the basilica of the saint in Assisi. His "Praises of the Most High" must be seen as a more theological counterpart of the "Canticle of Brother Sun." To juxtapose the two is to get a fuller, more faithful, spiritual portrait of the saint:

PRAISES OF THE MOST HIGH

You alone are holy, Lord God, wonder of wonders.

You are strong.

You are great.

You are the Most High.

You are omnipotent, Our Holy Father, Lord of Heaven and earth.

You, Lord God, one and three, are our every good.

You, Lord God, are good, all good, our highest good—Lord God living and true.

You are charity and love.

You are wisdom.

You are humility.

You are patience.

You are a firm anchor.

You are peace.

You are joy and happiness.

You are justice and temperance.

You are the fullness of riches.

You are beauty.

You are gentleness.

You are our protector.

You are our guardian and defender.

You are our strength.

You are refreshment.

You are our great hope.

You are our faith.

You are our most profound sweetness.

You are our eternal life, great and admirable Lord, Omnipotent God.

Holy and merciful Saviour!

The "Canticle of Brother Sun" directs our heart to God's creation, while the "Praises of the Most High" is oriented to God directly. Saint Francis wrote a third laud, very much in the spirit of the other two, which directs its attention to the personal strengths of the

God-searching person. This third laud adds another component to the thanks-filled life of the creature. The "Praises of Virtue" were written by Saint Francis to exalt the powers or strengths (that is what *virtue* literally means) that make the religious vision of life possible. These powers, as he says, are rooted in, and come forth from, God. They are the energies of the converted life.

THE PRAISES OF VIRTUE

I salute you, Regal Wisdom. May the Lord safeguard you with your holy sister, unsullied Simplicity.

Holy Lady Poverty! May the Lord watch over you and your sister, Holy Humility!

My pious Lady Charity! May the Lord watch over you and your holy sister, Obedience.

May the Lord protect all of you holy virtues, for you find your source in him and come forth from him.

No one in this world can possess you if he does not die to self.

He who possesses one of you, without offending the others, possesses all.

He who offends one of you lacks all and offends against all.

Each of you drives out vice and sin.

Holy Wisdom drives out Satan and his wiles.

Holy and pure Simplicity confounds the wisdom of this world and fleshly desires.

Holy Poverty drives out cupidity, avarice, and earthly desire.

Holy Humility overcomes pride, the men of the world, and all earthly things.

Holy Charity confounds all temptations of the flesh and the devil and all human fears.

Holy Obedience drives out carnal and bodily desires and keeps the body in check. It holds us subject to the Spirit and obedient to our brothers. It keeps us submissive to all the men of the world, and not only men but to the animals and flowers who can do what they want with us to the extent that God has given them power over us.

The perennial message, then, is to be found in Saint Francis's vision of the world as he saw it in faith. It is a vision that insists that we can be confident about our life in this world because the goodness of the Creator is refracted through creation in general and revelation in particular. We learn from creation and Christ. These two sources are nothing more than the traditional "two books" of medieval culture: the book of nature and the book of revelation.

The paradoxical message of Saint Francis is that the richness of this vision comes in proportion to our capacity to experience the poverty that gives us a sense of divine providence. A sense of this kind of poverty makes us grateful for the gift of creation, helps us to be sensitive to the needs of others, and allows us a closer identification with that Christ who became "poor for our sake."

The Franciscan message is timeless. Saint Francis did not reveal a new wisdom or search out a hidden *gnosis*. He went instinctively to the oldest of Christian sources: the sacramental life of the Church and the memory of Christ preserved in the Scriptures. It is the function of the saint to see the old in a new and pertinent way. For nearly a millennium before Saint Francis the Church, through its monks and ascetics, preserved the ancient faith against the onslaughts of barbarian anarchy and the general inertia of a dying civilization. Francis lived at a time when life was stirring in the cities, travel was on the increase, and mercantile life was vibrant. Europe was on the move. Francis provided a new way of reaching the now mobile populations of Europe. Francis took the simplicity of the Gospel to those masses. "What Saint Benedict stored," Chesterton once wrote, "Saint Francis scattered."

And, finally, the message of Saint Francis is timely. No age can be indifferent to the imperatives of beauty, compassion, mystery, love, self-sacrifice, and the heroic living of those virtues—least of all our age, which, in diverse ways and in hesitant steps, cries out for them. Saint Francis of Assisi, that very medieval man, is separated from us by eight centuries. Nonetheless, his life gives luminous insights into the meaning of words whose importance never lessens, no matter what the age.

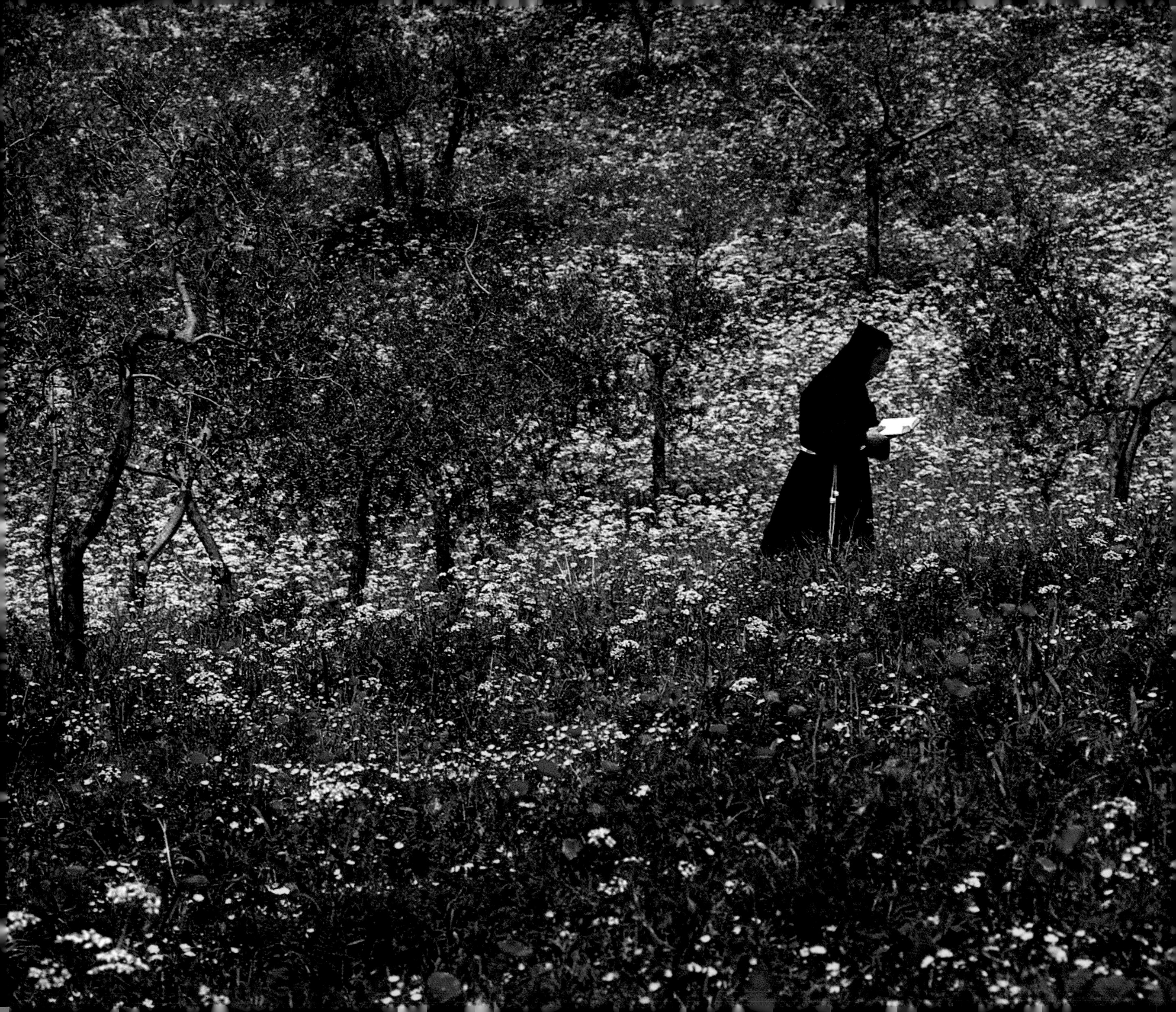

The Franciscan Revival

VISITORS to Assisi cannot but be struck by the huge numbers of people who come to the city. The casual tourist takes a quick tour of the most conspicuous sites associated with the life of Saint Francis and his mission: Saint Mary of the Angels in the valley below the town; and the fortresslike Romanesque basilica of the saint, where his tomb is located and where (in the upper church) there is a great cycle of frescoes, once attributed to Giotto himself, on the life of the saint and his miracles. More knowledgeable visitors will walk the medieval streets to visit the church of Saint Clare, and the wonderful little church and convent of San Damiano. If they are among the more hardy, they will walk up the winding road of Monte Subasio to visit the charming *Carceri*, the eremetical retreat often used by the saint. The countryside around the town attracts the eye of even the most jaded sightseer. The inevitable urban sprawl of modern Italy has not managed to obliterate the olive groves, the small pastures with their sea of blood red poppies in the spring, the snow white oxen, and all of the natural beauty that once entranced the saint himself and the painters of Umbria and Tuscany, who filled the backgrounds of their paintings with it. No one, I dare say, is ever disappointed by a visit to the city. It seems as beautiful as one imagined it. The novelist Evelyn Waugh, not given to easy emotions, once wrote to his wife that Assisi seemed filled with the grace of God.

The beauty of Assisi was not always so appreciated. In the late eighteenth century, the young Johann Wolfgang von Goethe made his "grand tour" of Italy. In his *Italienische Reise*, published in 1816, he describes a visit to Assisi. There was one thing he wanted to see there: a well preserved but not terribly significant Roman Temple, converted into a Christian church, which is in the main square of Assisi (one can see the temple in the background of Giotto's fresco of Saint Francis and his father before the Bishop of Assisi in the Bardi chapel of Santa Croce in Florence). Goethe evinced no interest in seeing the shrine of the saint or the art treasures of the basilica of Saint Francis. He quickly inspected the Roman temple and left the city posthaste.

Goethe was not alone in this indifference. He reflected an attitude that was shared by many intellectuals and critics in his own day, but which had roots going all the way back into the Renaissance period. By the sixteenth century, the great flush of Franciscan humanism had pretty well run its course outside the formal confines of the Church. Its considerable impact on the development of vernacular poetry had already been absorbed into the literary tradition. As urban capitalism became recognized as a vehicle for civic and cultural enrichment, its doctrine of poverty and simplicity of life had become irrelevant to large numbers of the intelligentsia. Petrarch's embrace of simplicity of life in the fourteenth century was replaced by the fifteenth-century humanist emphasis on the philanthropy of those who enhance the city with their wealth. The various branches of the Franciscan Orders continued to give yeoman service to the Church, but their influence on the larger culture was limited and their creativity sporadic. The exemplary power of the life of Saint Francis began to recede in European culture, to be replaced by the stereotype of the friar as a wandering troublemaker or a jovial and irrelevant *bon vivant*. The archetypical Franciscan of this kind was Friar Hubert in the *Canterbury Tales*. One could trace thousands of examples of this kind of friar from Chaucer to the time of the Reformation. Voltaire's gibe at Saint Francis and his followers is typically acerbic but not unexpected: "I am not overly pleased with that man Francis, who thought a real Christian should go begging in the street and wanted his sons, those robust lazybones, to take an oath to live at our expense."

One could hardly expect the savants and intellectuals of the seventeenth and eighteenth centuries to have been much charmed by the figure of Saint Francis of Assisi. They were passionate in their love of reason, while Francis had deep misgivings about the intellectual life. Their worldview was derived from the orderly physics of Newton while Francis believed, not in the Great Chain of Being, but in the fraternity of all of creation. Finally, as any close reader of Doctor Johnson or Henry Fielding knows, the eighteenth-century intellectuals had a great loathing for what they called religious "enthusiasm." If Henry Fielding could not stomach the English John Wesley, there was little chance that he was going to be charmed by the Italian Saint Francis. For the eighteenth-century intellectual taste there was something too primitive, too spontaneous, and too incipiently anarchical about the wandering Poor Man of Assisi.

The recovery of interest in Saint Francis in particular and Franciscanism in general outside the confines of institutional Roman Catholic culture was sparked by the Romantic concern for a less reasoned, more spontaneous view of both human nature and the emotional response of the human to the world of created nature. One can hardly imagine Alexander Pope admiring Saint Francis, but one has no trouble in thinking that William Blake—if he knew about the saint—would find him a congenial figure. In the same fashion, Francis would have been bewildered (and, one suspects, soon horrified) by the eighteenth-century notion of God being a "cosmic watchmaker," but may have found Matthew Arnold's notion of religion as "emotion tinged with morality" not totally reprehensible.

The nineteenth-century rediscovery of Saint Francis follows two tracks, the one poetic and the other historical. We shall briefly treat these subjects in turn even though, as is inevitable, there is some overlapping caused by the common romantic impulses behind both the poet's and historian's interest in the saint and his period.

One sees in the writings of some literary critics of the nineteenth century a rediscovery of the impact that Francis and his followers had on the development of vernacular poetry in the Middle Ages, especially in the Romance tongues. Antoine Ozanam's *Les Poetes Franciscans*, written in 1849, argued what is now a scholarly commonplace, namely, that Saint Francis and his friars triggered an outpouring of poetic sentiment in the various vernaculars on the continent. The same point was made a quarter of a century later by Matthew Arnold, in an essay on "Pagan and Medieval Religious Sentiment":

The beginnings of the mundane poetry of the Italians are in Sicily, at the court of the kings; the beginnings of their religious poetry are in Umbria with Saint Francis. His are the upper humble waters of a mighty stream; at the beginning of the thirteenth century it is Saint Francis, at the end, Dante. Now it happens that Saint Francis, too, like the Alexandrian songstress, has his hymn for the sun, our Adonis. *Canticle of the Sun, Canticle of the Creatures*—the poem goes by both names. Like the Alexandrian hymn, it is designed for popular use, but not for use by King Ptolemy's people; artless in language, irregular in rhythm, it matches with the childlike genius that produced it, and the simple natures that loved and repeated it . . .

The one English poet of the nineteenth century capable of writing poetry that directly reflected the Franciscan vision was, ironically, not a Franciscan but the Jesuit priest convert Gerard Manley Hopkins. Deeply influenced both by the romantic tradition of poetry in England and his own reading of Franciscan sources (mainly Saint Bonaventure and the Franciscan philosopher, William of Occam), Hopkins produced a body of poetry celebrating the presence of God and the echoes of Christ in the world of nature. Hopkins's sonnet "God's Grandeur" is a premier example of the Franciscan notion of God's detectable presence in the world of nature:

The world is charged with the grandeur of God.
It will flame out, like shining from shook foil;
It gathers to a greatness, like the ooze of oil
Crushed. Why do men then now not reck his rod?

Generations have trod, have trod, have trod;
And all is seared with trade; bleared, smeared with toil;
And wears man's smudge and shares man's smell; the soil
Is bare now, nor can foot feel, being shod.

And for all this, nature is never spent;
There lives the dearest freshness deep down things;
And through the last lights off the Black West went
Oh morning, at the brown brink eastward, springs—
Because the Holy Ghost over the bent
World broods with warm breast and with ah! bright wings.

Hopkins's intuition of the "dearest freshness deep down things" is a quintessentially Franciscan insight into the essential goodness of creation. In his great poem "That Nature is a Heraclitean Fire and of the Comfort of the Resurrection," Hopkins extends this insight to include the awareness of the human as participating in the very humanity of Christ. Out of the unpromising stuff of human flesh comes an awareness of Christ. Hopkins concludes his poem:

Across my foundering deck shone
A beacon, an eternal beam. / Flesh fade, and mortal trash
Fall to the residuary worm; / world's wildfire, leave but ash:
In a flash, at a trumpet crash,
I am all at once what Christ is / since he was what I am, and
This Jack, joke, poor potsherd / patch, matchwood, immortal diamond
Is immortal diamond.

The nineteenth-century historical interest in matters Franciscan derived from the search to define the nature of the Italian Renaissance. In 1860, the Swiss historian Jacob

Burckhardt published his magisterial study *The Civilization of the Renaissance in Italy*, a work that still defines the starting point of Renaissance historiography. Burckhardt argued that fifteenth-century Florentine culture marked a rebirth (literally, *renaissance*) of the long dormant classical culture of ancient Greece and Rome. It was in that century, he argued, that culture shifted its gaze from heaven to earth, insisting on the idea of individuality, and the desire for a state modeled on the cool rationality of Republican Rome. Burckhardt and his followers sharply distinguished the glittering worldly culture of the Renaissance from the world-denying heavenly city focused culture of the medieval period. It was a culture, they argued, that first put a high premium on the idea of fame and the immortalization of the self. The Renaissance, as they saw it, was rather like a flower blooming out of the ashes of a dead culture.

It was inevitable that Burckhardt's provocative ideas would be challenged and/or modified by subsequent historians. One obvious area of challenge would be to inquire whether or not it is plausible to posit a radical new cultural situation springing up instantly. Did the Renaissance, in fact, spring out of the medieval doldrums like Athena from the head of Zeus? To put the issue in another, more positive, way: what were the conditions in Italy that provided the Renaissance a matrix for its growth into a fully recognizable cultural phenomenon?

Henry Thode's *Franz von Assisi und Die Anfänge der Kunst in Italien*, written in 1885, argued that the art inspired by the life of Saint Francis gave to thirteenth- and fourteenth-century Italian art a forceful impetus that propelled it away from its rigid Italo-Byzantine mode into a fresh world that appreciated the lyrical beauty of the natural world. In other words, the humanistic spirit in the great art of fifteenth-century Florence was only possible because of the revolutionary character of the saint's life and the vision that devolved from it.

Thode's work emphasized the radical newness of Saint Francis. He saw the saint as a pivotal figure in cultural history. Saint Francis was the culmination of all that was noble in medieval culture and, more important, he was a harbinger of what was to come in the fresh new world of the fifteenth-century Renaissance. Thode's book was never particularly influential, but his portrait of the saint as a revolutionary figure would be taken up by Paul Sabatier in the last decade of the last century. Sabatier's life of the saint marks the beginning of serious Franciscan research. Whatever the defects and excesses of his research, Sabatier's portrait of Saint Francis was so provocative that even today one senses scholars disputing his ideas either explicitly or beneath the lines. (One sign of their unsettling character is that the Vatican put the biography on the *Index* of forbidden books.) For better or worse, Sabatier's view of Saint Francis colors much of Franciscan research and historiography right down to this day.

Sabatier's life of the saint was written in 1894. Since then, scholars have unearthed new sources of the saint's life that were not available then. Other Franciscanists have produced critical editions of the various *legenda*, done archival research in the period, and further clarified the cultural and religious history of the time. This outpouring of scholarship has prompted a steady stream of scholarly studies and new biographies of the saint. Raphael Brown's 1967 biography* cites some thirty-seven biographical studies following Sabatier's. Since Brown compiled his bibliography, there have been at least another half-dozen works published for the English speaking world.

Despite this impressive outpouring of scholarly and biographical writing, it is fair to say that no completely satisfactory life of Saint Francis yet exists. The reasons for this are hard to articulate. It may be that the questions raised by Sabatier still hang too heavily over the life of the saint. A completely fresh angle of writing on the saint is needed. Such a biography would require vast skills. It would demand a writer who had a thorough

---

*Reprinted at the end of *Omnibus of Sources*, ed. M. Habig (Chicago: Franciscan Herald Press, 1973).

grasp of the medieval milieu, a spirit of scholarly detachment from *parti pris* issues, a basic sympathy for the subject, and a sharply innovative and analytical mind. That such a book can be written seems plausible. One would like to see a scholar do for Saint Francis what Peter Brown has done for the great bishop of Hippo. Brown's 1967 work, *Saint Augustine of Hippo*, is a model of its genre. Whoever would write such a life of Saint Francis would serve the reading public well. One can hardly imagine a more challenging topic for a biographer.

The very enigmatic character of the life and personality of Saint Francis has challenged the imagination of the literary figure as much as the skills of the biographer. Literary works inspired by the saint, as one might suspect, tend to emphasize, not the orthodox Saint Francis, but the eccentric, revolutionary, or romantic one.

Hermann Hesse (winner of the Nobel Prize for Literature in 1946), under the influence of nineteenth-century romanticism, wrote a short monograph on Saint Francis of Assisi in 1904. In that same year he published his first novel, *Peter Camenzind*, which showed that his interest in Francis was not merely historical. The eponymous hero of the novel overcomes his disgust with the bohemian life of Zurich and Paris by a visit to Assisi, where he learns that the life of an artist can be enriched by the humanism he senses in the town and from the continuing influence of the saint. The example of Saint Francis serves as a paradigm who teaches the hero of the novel the value of suffering and love while encouraging him to cultivate a tender love for the world of nature around him. Finally, the self-centered life of the artist gives way to the caring service of others as he learns to nurture and befriend an ailing peasant named Boppi.

Hesse's novel was an attempt to describe a "cure" for artistic alienation. It was a theme that the novelist would pursue all of his life, although his philosophical and theological interests soon turned from the romantic Catholicism of Assisi to Eastern thought and personal involvement with Jungian analysis. The scope of that difference may be measured by a comparison of *Peter Camenzind* with the immensely popular

1927 novel *Siddhartha*, where the romantic Christianity of his early work has been totally sublimated.

For a far different fictional view of Saint Francis, one could consult *The Poor Man of God*, the fictionalized life of the saint written by the Greek novelist Nikos Kazantzakis.* Kazantzakis recalls, in his autobiographical memoir *Report to Greco*, how he made a visit to Assisi. It was there that he had a series of conversations with the famous Danish Franciscanist Johannes Joergensen that inspired him to write of the saint. Kazantzakis, true to the vitalist spirit he had learned as a student of Henri Bergson, was most interested in Francis the ascetic and searcher for God. Francis was the epitome of a soul who sought to transcend static religion for vital religion. His depiction of the life of Francis has little of the sentimentality that one finds in a novelist like Hesse or in the innumerable pious biographies of the saint. Francis is a ragged, lacerated figure who, as the novelist says, "writhed in the claws of God."

Kazantzakis's ascetic saint was not a mindless fanatic. It was his asceticism that set him free and ennobled him. He was a person who transmuted suffering and deprivation into pure goodness. Interestingly, Kazantzakis likens the saint to the great theologian and humanitarian Albert Schweitzer because of their mutual love of music, their unyielding reverence for all life, and their profound sense of human compassion. Saint Francis of Assisi and Albert Schweitzer, so different both in personality, culture, and theology, "take disease, hunger, cold, injustice, ugliness,—reality at its most horrible—and transubstantiate these into a reality yet more real where the wind of spirit blows. No, not of spirit; of love . . ."**

Hermann Hesse was interested in the "romantic" Saint Francis while Nikos Kazantzakis emphasized the ascetic saint. The Italian novelist Ignazio Silone never wrote about

*Written in 1951, the book was translated into English in 1960 and published under the title *Saint Francis*.
**Nikos Kazantzakis, *Report to Greco* (New York: Simon & Schuster, 1965), p. 379.

Saint Francis explicitly, but he was fascinated by the medieval revolutionary offspring of the saint. Silone argued that the Spiritual Franciscans left behind them a legacy of apocalyptic and revolutionary Catholicism which runs through the history of Italian Catholicism like a hidden stream. For Silone, the Church as an institution, the state in its several forms, and political parties (Silone, a staunch anti-Fascist, had been a founding member of the Italian Communist Party but broke with it in 1930), were all compromised by their fascination with power and its uses.

In the early novels, Silone depicted solitary individuals who fought against social oppression and for human solidarity. Silone's heroes, drawn with abundant references to the Gospels, were individual seekers who desired, as the hero of *Bread and Wine* said, to be saints even in their doubt and rebellion. For Silone these figures were not just reformers or utopian social critics; they were the manifestation of a kind of hidden religiousness that erupted into historical consciousness at times of crisis and human dislocation.

Silone's most explicitly Franciscan work was the 1968 play *The Story of a Humble Christian*. The central figure of the play was the medieval pope, Celestine V. Celestine was a pious and elderly hermit, a follower of the Spiritual Franciscans, who had resigned the papacy after only a few months in office. Dante deprecated Celestine in the *Inferno* for making the "great refusal" that allowed the poet's mortal enemy, Boniface VIII, to ascend the chair of Peter. For Silone, Celestine's beauty was to be found precisely in his momentous refusal. Celestine's rejection of power was a "counter sign" of poverty and love rendering prophetic judgment on the wealth, power, and worldliness of the medieval papacy. For Silone, Celestine stood as a high mark in the subterranean tradition of the Spiritual Franciscans of the Middle Ages who unremittingly battled the worldly pretensions of the Church. History has labeled the Spirituals as heretical and sectarian; Silone lauds them as prophetic and timely.

The spirit of Saint Francis lives in more ways than as an inspiration for the literary imagination. Within the Roman Catholic Church, the various branches of the Franciscan Order claim kinship with the saint and his first friars. The First Order is made up of friars (from the Latin *fratres*—brothers) who historically derive from the original Franciscans, though with some historical modifications. Within the First Order are the Friars Minor (O.F.M.), the Friars Minor Conventual (O.F.M. Conv.), and the Capuchins (O.F.M. Cap.), the latter a reform group of Franciscans whose origins date to the Counter Reformation. The various branches of the First Order serve the Church in parishes, schools, chaplaincies, foreign missions, and other apostolic works within the Catholic tradition. For centuries the friars have been the custodians of the shrines in the Holy Land, a task that powerfully reminds us of Saint Francis's deep love for the Middle East and his various missionary excursions to that part of the world.

The Second Order of Saint Francis is made up of those women religious who, in honor of their founder, are called Poor Clares. They are a cloistered order of women contemplatives who devote their lives to solitude, prayer, and penance.

The Third Order, founded by Saint Francis, consists of those who live in the world as layfolk but try to follow the Franciscan style of life according to their station and place in life. Saint Francis wrote a rule of life for such persons that is now lost. We do possess a variation of that lost rule written by Cardinal Hugolin (later Pope Gregory IX), which has been modified over the course of the centuries to accommodate the exigencies of changing cultural and social conditions. Some religious groups have sought to follow this way of life in a more formally religious and communitarian fashion. There is a Third Order Regular (T.O.R.) of priests and brothers. Many religious orders of sisters in the Catholic Church put themselves under the patronage of Saint Francis and adopt the rule of the Third Order as their rule of life.

The Franciscan charism is not limited to those groups who identify themselves formally as Franciscans within the Roman Catholic Church. There have been Anglican Franciscans, both male and female, since the nineteenth century. Interestingly, the Anglican Franciscans did not start within the High Church circles of Anglicanism but in the more evangelical wing of the Anglican church, where strong sentiments of social conscience developed during the heyday of the Industrial Revolution. There are still small religious groups of Anglican Franciscans both in this country and Great Britain.

Within the Roman Catholic tradition there are also manifestations of the Franciscan spirit outside the formal Franciscan family of friars and sisters. The spirit of the Catholic Worker Movement is heavily dependent on the Franciscan notion of living in poverty. With their strong tradition of pacifism, their identification with the poor, and their simple insistence on Gospel values, the Catholic Workers may be the clearest example in our time of what the original Franciscans hoped to accomplish in the world. Their very existence in the complex world of urban civilization testifies strongly to the vitality of the Franciscan spirit. The Catholic Workers attempt to live out the ideals of the saint without any historical intent to do things the way they were done in the thirteenth century, or with any *parti pris* claims of lineal ancestry with the original Franciscan spirit.

Saint Francis was a person of his own age who speaks to all ages. It is difficult to see him clearly through the veils of time, legend, and sentiment, but we still desire to know more about him. It is not all that hard to see why. Any sensitive person today knows that the global problems of contemporary society orbit around issues of international peace, world hunger, exhaustion of resources, and spoliation of the natural environment. To these problems, the religious person worries about the gradual, but seemingly inexorable, erosion of belief. To all of these issues Saint Francis has something profound to say. Anyone with insight into the very vexatious problems of the day deserves a hearing. That may just be the reason why Saint Francis is, as Sabatier noted nearly a century ago, one of those figures who belongs not to the Church, but to the world:

When one reaches these heights, he no longer belongs to a sectarian movement: he belongs to humanity. He is like those miracles of nature that chance had given to this or that land but which in reality belong to all people, for they are the common and inalienable property of all. Homer, Shakespeare, Dante, Goethe, Rembrandt, and Michelangelo belong to all of us, as do the ruins of Greece and Rome. Or better, they belong to all those who love or understand them the best.

But that which is a truism when one speaks of men of reason or geniuses of the imagination becomes a paradox when one speaks of religious genius. The church has laid such a claim on them that it appears that she owns them by some sort of right. It cannot be that this act of confiscation will endure forever. To stop it an act of demolition or negation is hardly necessary. Let them have their chapels and relics, and, far from denigrating the saints, let us exalt them in all their true grandeur.

For Further Reading

The Life of Saint Francis

Thomas of Celano's description, like his *Legenda* in general, is idealized. That should not surprise us. The early Franciscan writers wished to put forth Saint Francis as a model of the following of Christ. They wished to interpret Saint Francis for their readers. What the thirteenth-century writers did in their time is not unlike the modern efforts to understand the saint and make his life intelligible for the age.

Paul Sabatier's *Vie de Saint François d'Assise* (Paris: Fischbacker, 1894; also in English translation but now out of print) depicted Francis as a religious revolutionary whose life was a form of religious revival. According to Sabatier, the intentions of Francis were frustrated by the Church, which turned his simple style of life into a legalistically founded religious order. Sabatier's thesis has been much debated (his work was put on the *Index* by the Catholic Church), but is still influential. Johannes Joergensen's *Saint Francis of Assisi* (Garden City: Doubleday Image, 1955) was a response to Sabatier's book as well as one of the most popular lives of the saint ever written. Gilbert Keith Chesterton's *Saint Francis of Assisi* (Garden City: Doubleday Image, 1957) is typically Chestertonian. It is cavalier with facts and historical sequence, but brilliant in its interpretation of the saint's significance. Chesterton emphasizes the poetry, simplicity, and evangelical fervor of the saint. The Greek novelist Nikos Kazantzakis's *Saint Francis* (New York: Simon & Schuster, 1962) is a highly fictionalized account of the saint's life (and his relationship to Saint Clare), which underscores Francis as a God-intoxicated ascetic. It is a welcome, if lopsided, corrective to overly sentimental versions of his life. Omer Englebert's *Saint Francis of Assisi* (Chicago: Franciscan Herald, 1965) falls victim to that gush so often found in writings about the saint, but it is based on serious scholarship and has valuable bibliographies appended to the book. The Anglican bishop John Moorman has been a keen student of Franciscanism. Moorman's *A History of the Franciscan Order* (New York: Oxford University Press, 1968) has a fine scholarly life of the saint in the opening chapters of that very valuable study. John Holland Smith's *Saint Francis of Assisi* (New York: Scribner's, 1973) is a reliable unfolding of the saint's life, but his interpretation of that life bogs down in rather murky Jungian generalizations.

For those who wish to read such early sources as Thomas of Celano and Bonaventure on the life of Saint Francis, *Saint Francis of Assisi: English Omnibus of the Sources for the Life of Saint Francis*, edited by Marion Habig (Chicago: Franciscan Herald, 1973) is an exhaustive and indispensable source. It contains all of the major legends and the writings of the saint with copious notes, bibliographies, and chronologies. *Brother Francis: Writings by and about Saint Francis of Assisi*, edited by Lawrence Cunningham (New York: Harper & Row, 1972), is a mosaic of early and contemporary writings about the saint.

Two recent books, appearing on the eve of the 800th anniversary celebrations commemorating the birth of the saint, deserve mention. Arnaldo Fortini's *Francis of Assisi*, translated by Helen Moak (New York: Crossroad, 1980), is an English adaptation of the massive five volume Italian original. Fortini was the long time mayor of Assisi and his knowledge of historical and archival material is staggering. Fortini's biography, despite its rather baroque style, is an indispensable work for understanding the saint's historical milieu. Adolf Holl's *The Last Christian: A Biography of Francis of Assisi* (Garden City, New York: Doubleday, 1980) is an attempt to interpret Francis as a radically revolutionary figure in the history of Christianity.

Lady Poverty and Mother Earth

Edward A. Armstrong's *Saint Francis: Nature Mystic* (Berkeley: University of California Press, 1973) is an extremely interesting study of the folklore motifs behind the stories of Saint Francis and his love for animals and the natural world. Lynn White's often-anthologized article "The Historical Roots of Our Ecological Crisis," *Science* (1967), pp. 1203–07, studies Saint Francis's attitude towards nature and proposes him as the patron saint of the ecological movement.

Malcolm Lambert's *Franciscan Poverty* (London: S.P.C.K., 1961) is a fundamental historical study of the interpretation of poverty in early Franciscanism. E. Randolph Daniels's *The Franciscan Concept of Mission in the High Middle Ages* (Lexington: University of Kentucky Press, 1975) attempts to focus attention away from poverty as a central motif in understanding early Franciscanism with some success. Cajetan Esser's *The Origins of the Franciscan Order* (Chicago: Franciscan Herald, 1970) is a rigorous study by one of the outstanding Franciscan scholars of this age.

A completely satisfactory study of Franciscan spirituality is yet to be written. Works like Ignatius Brady, ed., *The Marrow of the Gospel* (Chicago: Franciscan Herald, 1958) and A. Van Corstanje's *The Covenant with God's Poor* (Chicago: Franciscan Herald, 1966) are of some interest. Some of the most insightful ideas about poverty in our time have been written by (and lived by) the late Dorothy Day; one can consult William D. Miller's *A Harsh and Dreadful Love: Dorothy Day and the Catholic Worker Movement* (Garden City, New York: Doubleday Image, 1973), as well as Professor Miller's forthcoming biography of Dorothy Day (San Francisco: Harper & Row).

The Franciscan Revival

David Jeffrey's *The Early English Lyric and Franciscan Spirituality* (Lincoln: University of Nebraska Press, 1975) is an excellent study of the impact of Franciscanism on the development of medieval lyric poetry in English. George Kaftal's *Saint Francis in Italian Painting* (Florence: Sansoni, 1955) is a fine introduction to the impact of Francis on the visual arts of the thirteenth and fourteenth centuries. Hans Baron's essay "Franciscan Poverty and Civic Wealth as Factors in the Development of Humanstic Thought," *Speculum* 3 (1938), is a seminal study of the decline of Franciscan influence in the early Renaissance. Rosalind Brooke's *Early Franciscan Government: From Elias to Bonaventure* (Cambridge: University of Cambridge Press, 1959) is a brilliant exposition of the evolution of early Franciscanism. Lawrence S. Cunningham's *Saint Francis of Assisi* (Boston: Twayne, 1976) attempts to survey the revival of Franciscan studies from the nineteenth century on. Ignatius Brady's *The Legends and Writings of Saint Clare of Assisi* (Olean, New York: Franciscan Sources, 1953) is a fundamental source for an appreciation of Saint Clare.

Chronology

1181/1182

While the rich merchant Pietro Bernardone was away in France on business, his wife, Pica, gave birth to a son in Assisi and christened him Giovanni. But his father called the boy Francesco, in honor of France, and this was the name by which Francis was known for the rest of his life.

1193/1194

Birth of Chiara Favarone, later Saint Clare, founder of the Order of the Poor Clares.

1202

In the autumn, Francis fought in a battle between Assisi and Perugia, which ended in the defeat of Assisi. Francis was taken prisoner.

1203

After a year in prison in Perugia, Francis returned to Assisi in poor health.

1
Assisi. View of the city.

1204

Francis decided to go to Apulia as a knight in the army of Gualtieri di Brienne, who, as a delegate of Pope Innocent III, was successful in his fight against the German princes in defense of the pope's political interests. But by the time Francis reached nearby Spoleto his doubts, kindled in him by dreams and unsettling visions, got the better of his initial military resolve. Francis returned to Assisi.

1205

In June, Francis took part for the last time in a "serenade"—a lively banquet with young friends who belonged to the Company of the Tripudianti, or carousers. The festivities of this group, which included songs and dances, constituted the principal amusements for the young people of Assisi. Bernardone's rich and popular son was often proclaimed "king of the feast."

1206

After his return from Rome, Francis regularly visited the leprosarium of San Lazzaro, near Assisi. In late autumn, while absorbed in prayer in the half-ruined little church of San Damiano, he heard Christ speaking to

2

Assisi. Cathedral of San Ruffino.

him from the wooden cross above the altar: "Francis, go and restore my house, which, as you see, is going to ruin." Francis took the command literally, and sold off some bolts of cloth from his father's firm to procure the money necessary to restore San Damiano.

3

Sonare et ballare. Medieval manuscript in the Biblioteca Casanatense, Rome.

1207

The sale of these bolts of cloth infuriated Pietro Bernardone, who locked his son up at home. In February, Pietro left Assisi on business and his wife released Francis, consoling him and attempting to convince the boy to obey his father. But Francis returned to San Damiano immediately and began restoring the little church. His father then brought suit against Francis before the Bishop of Assisi. Francis publicly renounced his paternal inheritance and broke off all relationship with his father.

1207/1208

Francis first moved to Gubbio, where he worked as an orderly in the leprosarium. He soon returned to Assisi, where he went about begging for stones, lime, and money to be used in restoring the chapels of San Damiano, San Pietro, and the Porziuncola. On February 24, 1208, as Francis listened in the Chapel of the Porziuncola to the Gospel according to Matthew, chapter 10, he understood his future mission: "Christ sends forth his disciples and bids them to announce in every place that the Kingdom of Heaven is at hand."

1208

In March, dressed in a habit of sackcloth belted by a piece of rope, Francis preached in public for the first time. On April 16 a local nobleman, Bernardo Quintavalle, gave all his wealth to the poor and joined the company of Francis. During that spring other men joined the group and traveled as lay missionaries to the Marches. In summer, they returned to Assisi and lived in the forest of the Porziuncola. In autumn the brotherhood, which had grown even larger, set out upon a second pilgrimage of preaching.

1209

In spring, Francis and his companions made a pilgrimage to Rome. There Pope Innocent III granted verbal approval of the First Rule, which advocated living strictly according to the Gospel, and conceded to the itinerant friars the right to preach. On their return to Assisi, they settled at Rivo Torto, where they were joined by their first ordained priest, Brother Silvestro.

1210

For practical reasons, the Brothers had to leave their little hut at Rivo Torto. Francis obtained from the Benedictines of Monte Subiaco permission to use the little church of Santa Maria degli Angeli, in Porziuncola, and to build a hut nearby. Thus Porziuncola became the first home of the Franciscan Order.

4

Assisi. Temple of Minerva.

1211

Francis and Brother Rufino, cousin of Chiara Favarone, preached half-naked in the Cathedral of Assisi. Chiara, only seventeen, insisted on being introduced to Francis by Rufino. She and Francis met frequently thereafter, even though Chiara was aware that Francis was considered to be ridiculous and slightly crazy by conventional Assisi society.

5
Gubbio. View of the town.

1212

On the evening of Palm Sunday Chiara, accompanied by her faithful cousin Pacifica, left home to join Francis in the Porziuncola forest. She cut her long fair hair, donned the Franciscan habit, and accepted the rule of Francis and his companions. For some weeks she hid in the Benedictine monastery of San Paolo, near Bastia, until Francis turned over to her the church of San Damiano as a permanent home. She was accompanied there by her younger sister, Agnes, and Pacifica, and was later joined by her sister Beatrice, her mother, Ortolana, and a number of girls of noble families. This was the claustral community of San Damiano, which later became the Order of the Poor Clares.

1212

In later summer, Francis left Assisi with the intention of visiting the birthplace of Christ. But winds and storms were too much for his ship, which was grounded on the Dalmatian coast. Francis returned to Italy, probably to Ancona, where he began another preaching pilgrimage in the Marches.

1213

On May 8 Count Orlando di Chiusi legally ceded to Francis and his brotherhood the use of Mount Verna, in eastern Tuscany, in perpetuity. At Pentecost, the first general assembly of the Franciscan Brotherhood, which by then had rapidly increased in numbers, was held at the Porziuncola.

1214

After the second assembly of Pentecost (which was later called the Chapter), Francis left for Spain with the intention of proceeding to Morocco to bring the Gospel to the Muslims. It is possible that he first went to Santiago de Campostella, one of the most celebrated pilgrimage churches of Christianity at that time. But illness forced Francis to renounce his Moroccan project and return to Porziuncola. Meanwhile, other brothers joined the group, many of them noble and learned. Among them was Thomas of Celano, who later became the first biographer of Saint Francis of Assisi.

1215

Francis went to Rome, where he took part in the Fourth Lateran Council. It is possible that his first encounter with Saint Dominic, founder of the Dominican order, took place at that time.

6

Francis Presents His Rule of the Minor Friars to Pope Innocent III; Upper Church of Saint Francis, Assisi; Giotto.

7

Detail from *Saint Clare and Scenes from Her Life*; Church of Saint Clare, Assisi; Anonymous (13th century).

1216

On July 16, Pope Innocent III died in Perugia. Two days later Cardinal Cencio Savelli was elected and took the name Honorius III. Cardinal James of Vitry was present at the election, and in October of the same year he wrote a letter to a friend in Lorraine in which he mentions the *Fratres Minores* of Francis. It is quite possible that he met Francis in Perugia, but it is in any case certain that it was there that he learned of the brotherhood. This is the first historic document we have which refers to the Friars Minor.

1217

The annual Pentecost Chapter of the Porziuncola had by now become a tradition. This year the first organizational structures of the order were formulated. Saint Dominic was present as a guest. Pietro di Catania was nominated vicar of Francis. The brotherhood was divided into "provinces," and to each was given a "provincial ministry." Friar Egidio was sent to Tunisia, Friar Elia to Syria, others to Germany and Hungary. Francis was on his way to France, but Cardinal Hugolin of Ostia in Florence convinced him to remain in Italy.

1218

Francis was asked to preach to Pope Honorius III and to the Cardinals of the Holy College. Hugolin of Ostia, who by the request of Francis was nominated Protector of the Franciscan Brotherhood, delivered to Francis a carefully composed manuscript, in perfect Latin, for him to use as his sermon. But once in the pulpit, the sermon learned by heart vanished from his memory, and Francis instead delivered an extemporaneous sermon in Tuscan vulgate, in which the haughtiness and bad example of the clergy were chastised as scandals of the Church. As a result, the pope issued the bull *"Cum dilecti,"* in which bishops were assured of the orthodoxy of the Friars Minor and of their zealous Christianity, and were encouraged to relax their previous reserve.

1219

Following the Pentecost Chapter, during which new missions were decided, Francis embarked, on June 24, from Ancona, on a ship that was to take him near the Egyptian city of Damietta, under siege by an army of Crusaders. Disgusted by the immorality and cruelty of the Christian army, Francis

decided to visit the sultan Melek-el-Kamel, who received him with cordial hospitality. The discussions they had about religion and peace during Francis's eight-day visit left a strong impression on the sultan, though no tangible results were forthcoming. Francis returned to the Christian camp and witnessed the bloodbath perpetuated by the Crusaders on November 5, during the conquest of Damietta. He left towards the end of the year for Akka, in Syria, where he met Friar Elia and Friar Pietro da Catania.

8
The cloister of San Damiano.

1220

Word was received that five brothers were killed in Morocco, the first martyrs of the Order. It is possible that Francis and his two companions managed to reach the Holy Land. He returned to Italy, landing at Venice. The brotherhood, having grown to comprise thousands of adherents, was plagued by tension and confusion. At the Chapter of Pentecost, Francis left the direction of the Order to Pietro da Catania. On September 20, in consideration of the need for greater discipline, the pope required that new brothers undergo a novitiate before acceptance.

9

The Franciscan sanctuary of La Verna as it appears today.

1221

On March 1, Pietro da Catania died. During the Pentecost Chapter, with the participation of over five thousand brothers gathered at the Porziuncola, Friar Elia da Cortona was elected (on the proposal of Francis) to preside over the brotherhood. The brotherhood was becoming more and more like a religious order, and a modified Rule, proposed by Francis, was approved by the majority of the Chapter. This Rule is known as the Second Rule (the text of Francis's First Rule has not survived). The Second Rule is also called the Unconfirmed Rule because the pope, supported by Cardinal Hugolin, had refused his approval. In autumn, however, the pope approved the rule of the Brothers of Penance, later to become the Third Order (or Tertiaries).

1222

Early in the year, Francis preached in Southern Italy and probably stayed as a guest in Emperor Federick II's castle near Bari. At the beginning of summer he returned to Umbria, and on August 15 gave a sermon in the main square in Bologna.

1223

Cardinal Hugolin begged Francis to modify the Second Unconfirmed Rule. Francis retired with Brother Leo to the hermitage of Fonte Colombo (near Rieti). Cardinal Hugolin further modifed Francis's text, giving it the wording that was finally approved on November 29 by Pope Honorious III as the Definite Rule (Confirmed Rule). Francis, dejected, sought consolation in a cave near Greccio where, together with the peasants and shepherds and their animals, he organized a crèche to celebrate Christmas.

1224

Francis had been aware for some time of his increasing physical weakness (today it is believed that he suffered from some kind of cancer); he was also subject to severe bouts of depression. He reacted by retiring into mystical prayer. In late summer he went to La Verna where, on September 14 or 15, he

10

Francis Preaching Before Pope Honorius III; Upper Church of Saint Francis, Assisi; Giotto.

had an ecstatic vision of Christ on the cross and received the Stigmata, the five wounds of the Crucified Christ. In December, Francis set off riding a donkey for his last preaching pilgrimage through Umbria and the Marches.

1225

As his pilgrimage progressed, his eyesight continued to worsen, and he stopped for the summer in the garden of San Damiano, where he was lovingly cared for by Clare. During this stay he wrote the "Canticle of

11

Greccio. The site of the first crèche, as it appears today.

Brother Sun." In August, he underwent an operation on his eyes in Rieti, but the efforts of several doctors were unsuccessful. With weakening eyesight, and ever worsening health, Francis was received by the Bishop of Rieti in his palace.

1226

In spring, following the advice of his doctors, Francis moved from Rieti to Siena for further medical care. On the return journey he stopped off in Cortona, where he composed his final Testament. Since his health was getting worse, the brothers took him to the Bishop of Assisi's castle. But when Francis felt close to dying, he asked to be carried to the Porziuncola. Leaving Assisi, he gave the town his last blessing. He ordered his brothers to lay him down naked, without any of his belongings, "on the naked earth." He died on the night between October 3 and 4, 1226.

1228

On March 19, 1227, Cardinal Hugolin of Ostia, until then the Protector of Francis and his brotherhood, was elected pope with the name of Gregory IX. Only a year later he issued a bull, *"Recolentes,"* in which he asked for donations to be collected in order to build a large basilica in Assisi, in honor of Francis. Two months later he went to Assisi, and on July 19, 1228 he proclaimed the canonization of Francis. A short while later he entrusted to Thomas of Celano the task of writing a biography of Saint Francis.

1230

On May 25, Francis's body was moved to the crypt of the new Basilica di San Francesco. On September 28, the pope issued a bull, *"Quo Elongati,"* which stated that it was not compulsory for the members of the Order to follow Saint Francis's will and testament literally, and interpreted the concept of poverty, as stated in the "Definitive Rule" of 1223 in a more moderate way.

1253

Clare, who meanwhile had become abbess through ecclesiastical law, nevertheless remained pledged to Francis's concept of poverty and devoted to his ideals. She strongly opposed all pressures put upon her, and submitted to Pope Innocent IV the Rule that she herself had compiled, in which she advocated the unconditional pledge to Holy Poverty just as she had promised to God and to Saint Francis. The pope gave in to what can be considered her ultimatum, and confirmed Clare's Rule in Assisi on August 9, 1253. Two days later, on August 11, Clare died. She was canonized by Pope Alexander IV in August 1255.

12
Façade of the Upper Church of Saint Francis, Assisi.

Color Plate Captions

Page 2

"Francis Preaching to the Birds," detail from the panel painting *Saint Francis and Scenes from his Life*; Church of Saint Francis, Pescia; Bonaventura Berlinghieri.

3

A field of sunflowers near Todi.

4

Detail of sheep from *The Sacrifice of Joachim* (fresco); Arena Chapel, Padua; Giotto.

5

Umbrian shepherd with his flock in the "Great Plain" of Castelluccio, near Norcia.

6

Detail of horse from *Francis Gives his Cloak to a Poor Knight* (fresco); Upper Church of Saint Francis, Assisi; Giotto.

7

Early morning Umbrian scene, with donkey.

8

Evening wood at Monteluco where Francis founded, in 1218, one of his first communities.

17–24

Portraits of Saint Francis, painted ca. 1228–1328. (See p. 16.)

41

The Birth of Francis and *A Simpleton Renders Homage to Francis*, two scenes illustrating the fifteenth-century legend that Francis was born in a stable. The artist's setting of Francis's birth in a manger is obviously allegorical. (Continuing the legend, the third scene depicts Christ, disguised as a beggar, visiting the Bernardone household at the birth of Francis. Benozzo Gozzoli.

42

A Simpleton Renders Homage to the Young Francis in the Square of Assisi, Spreading His Cloak for Him to Walk On; Upper Church of Saint Francis, Assisi; Giotto.

43

Francis Gives His Clothes to His Father as a Sign of His Complete Renunciation of Earthly Goods (the Saint is standing next to Guido, Bishop of Assisi, who has covered him with his cloak; the incensed father is held back by the nobles as Francis points to heaven, where his true Father resides); Church of Santa Croce, Florence; Giotto.

44

Detail from *The Crucifix in San Damiano Exhorts Francis to Restore the Church*; Upper Church of Saint Francis, Assisi; Giotto.

45

Detail from the fresco *Francis with the Wolf of Gubbio*; Church of Saint Francis, Pienza; Anonymous (14th century).

46

Francis Before the Sultan; Church of Santa Croce, Florence; Giotto.

47

Francis, Together with Another Brother, Preaching to the Birds; Lower Church of Saint Francis, Assisi; Saint Francis Master (13th century).

48

Francis Receives the Stigmata; Church of Santa Croce, Florence; Giotto.

49

Detail from *Saint Francis in Ecstasy*; Frick Collection, New York; Giovanni Bellini.

Index